Tales of a Helicopter Pilot

TALES OF A Helicopter PILOT

★ ★ ★ ★ ★ ★ ★ ★ ★ ★ ★ ★ ★ ★

RICHARD C. KIRKLAND

Smithsonian Institution Press • Washington and London

Copy editor: Robert A. Poarch
Designer: Jody Billert

Library of Congress Cataloging-in-Publication Data
Kirkland, Richard C.
Tales of a helicopter pilot / Richard C. Kirkland.
p. cm.
ISBN 1-56098-952-1 (alk. paper)
1. Kirkland, Richard C.—Anecdotes. 2. Helicopter pilots—United States—Anecdotes.
3. Helicopters in search and rescue operations—Anecdotes. I. Title.
TL540.K52 A3 2001
629.132′5252—dc21 2001032213

British Library Cataloguing-in-Publication Data is available

Manufactured in the United States of America
07 06 05 04 03 02 5 4 3 2 1

♾ The paper used in this publication meets the minimum requirements of the American National Standard for Information Sciences—Permanence of Paper for Printed Library Materials ANSI Z39.48-1984.

To my wife, Maria, and all our children and grandchildren:
Richard, Cindy, Roger, Kathleen, Candace, Jeff, Andrea, Stephanie,
Alden, John, Barbara, Scott, Jo, Michael, Kevin, Michele, Kris,
Allison, Wesley, Aria, Mina, Ferrel, Alexis, Bella, Adrienne,
Gwyneth, Nathaniel, and Sophia Rose.

And to Robert Heinrich, helicopter pilot and man of honor.

Contents

Preface

It was satisfying to have readers call me or send me an E-mail saying how much they enjoyed my first book, *Tales of a War Pilot,* and asking if I was going to write another book. I got to thinking about it and realized that I had only scratched the surface of the many experiences associated with my half century of flying. I asked the folks at Smithsonian Institution Press, and they liked the idea. So I decided to write a book of true stories about the history and the characters involved with the most exciting flying machine of all: the helicopter.

Not long ago the aviation world considered the whirlybird a novelty of little practical use. Today it plays a role in many areas of both commercial and military aviation, and its life-saving capacity is unmatched. The helicopter creates its own excitement and adventure. In an airplane, you take off, go to your destination, and land. In a helicopter, there is no telling where you may be called upon to go, where you might land, or whose life you may snatch from the jaws of death.

Since I began my helicopter flying not long after America's first helicopter (the Sikorsky) was produced, I have witnessed rotary-wing evolution from its primitive beginning to the current advanced technology. It was a long, fascinating journey, from which I have selected diverse and often dramatic stories, in both war and peace.

Tales of a Helicopter Pilot includes my experiences and those of others, during the early days of helicopter flying in the United States Army and Air Force, and in the many civil applications that followed as the helicopter matured and took its rightful place in the aviation world.

The stories are all taken from true incidents and involve first-generation to present-day helicopter technology. My objective is to present the excitement and drama, while providing an earthy picture of historic characters and events. I recreated dialogue wherever I could, because it tells the story in an interesting way and gives the reader additional insight into the ambiance and the jargon. The dialogue is my interpretation of how a particular situation transpired, based on personal knowledge and historical facts. I used the characters' real names, except for a couple of sensitive cases.

I counted on my years of helicopter experience to give me the insight and perspective to improvise where necessary in the narrations, while maintaining historical accuracy. Where I lacked certain information or needed to substantiate dates, places, and names, I consulted the Helicopter Foundation International Archives in Alexandria, Virginia.

1

First Flight

The squadron ready room would normally be deserted on a Friday afternoon in these post–World War II days, so I was surprised to walk in and see it packed with pilots milling around, talking, and smoking.

"What's going on, John?" I asked a tall, fresh-faced second lieutenant.

"Oh hi, sir. Didn't you get the word?"

"What word?"

"About the mandatory formation. It's a good thing you got here, 'cause the colonel ordered all pilots to report to the hangar four ramp at fifteen hundred hours. We're just getting ready to go."

"That's just like our great commander to call a formation on Friday afternoon. Well, as much as I know he'll miss me, I'm not going to his little shindig," I growled.

The young officer's eyes widened. "But . . . but, sir . . . it's mandatory!"

I looked at the new second lieutenant who had only recently graduated from the rigorous discipline of cadet flight training and was still gung ho on military discipline. "Okay, John, what's this formation all about, do you know?"

"Captain Wall says we're gonna see a helicopter demonstration."

"A helicopter?"

"Yeah, it's the first one ever to land here. Captain Wall says it's gonna be assigned to our outfit. Have you ever seen one?"

I shook my head.

"Me either, but I'm kinda curious to see it, aren't you?"

I shook my head again.

No. I wasn't interested in seeing a helicopter. All I wanted to see was a jet, with me at the controls. I wanted desperately to fly the new jets. In fact, that was the primary reason I had elected to stay in the Army Air Forces after the war was over. I loved flying the World War II fighters, particularly the P-38, which I had flown in combat against the Japanese Zero. But my burning desire now was to fly the new Lockheed P-80 jet.

The U.S. military faced a big problem at the conclusion of World War II. They had all these war machines and people they didn't know what to do with. Most wanted out as soon as possible; they had had enough of military life and war, and you sure couldn't blame them. But sorting it all out was not easy. I think our leaders did as well as they could under the circumstances, but it was still a big mess.

Anyway, as one of those who wanted to stay in, I ended up at McChord Army Air Forces Base, Washington, in a sort of catch-all squadron with an assortment of leftover war birds. Our official mission was air and sea search and rescue—and anything else command could think of.

The colonel in charge of this assortment had spent the war at a stateside training base and developed some kind of complex because he didn't have a lot of medals. Unfortunately, I was wearing my class-A uniform the day I first reported to him. When he eyed my decorations, I knew the die was cast. Each time I submitted a request for jet school, he sent it back disapproved. I would immediately submit another one, since I was determined. But he was just as determined, and he was a colonel and I was a first lieutenant.

"You don't want to see the helicopter?" John asked, disappointed.

"No. . . . Not really, John. What I want to see around here is a P-80 jet, and I . . ."

"All right, let's go!" Captain Wall, our unit commander, suddenly barked above the noise in the ready room. "And I want everyone present; no goofing off."

I glanced at John and shrugged. "What the heck, let's go see the helicopter. I don't have anything better to do anyway."

Although attendance was mandatory, the formation on the flight ramp at hangar four was informal, somewhat out of character for the colonel, who usually required strict military protocol on such occasions. The senior officers gathered in one group, while the juniors, dressed in a mixture of uniforms and flight suits, milled around in satellites.

At precisely fifteen hundred hours, an olive drab, war-vintage staff car pulled up to the flight-ramp entrance at hangar number four. The driver leaped out and swung open the back door. The colonel, dressed in his class-A uniform, stepped out briskly.

One of the senior officers sang out: "Ten-hut!" The milling group came to loose attention. The colonel stood for a moment silently surveying the group of pilots, who stood staring back at him. As was his custom, he wore his service cap pulled down low over his eyes. The gold braid atop the visor glistened in stark contrast to the darkened underside, where his narrowed eyes zeroed in on me.

"All right, gentlemen," he finally announced. "You may stand at ease. I've called you here to observe a *heeleocopter* flight demonstration. This aircraft, or whatever you want to call it, is a Sikorsky R-5, which will be assigned to our air-and-sea search-and-rescue function at this station. This thing is supposed to come save you if you go down in the boonies. I doubt anyone here has ever seen one of these contraptions fly, and I'm not convinced that it does."

The colonel paused in consideration of a trickling of decorous laughter. "Anyway, we're stuck with it, so we're gonna watch it do its thing, by order of headquarters."

I smiled to myself. I knew now why the informal formation. It was the colonel's way of degrading a HQ order that, for whatever neurotic reason, he did not like. But then the commander's prejudices were consistent and dependable.

Before I saw it, I heard it: a sound totally alien to anything I had ever heard around an airfield. It wasn't like the deep crack of an Allison or a Rolls-Royce engine, or even like the roar of the new jets. It was a whirling, beating sound—somewhat like that of a thrashing machine.

When the helicopter appeared over the tree line at the opposite end of the airfield, it looked like some kind of a gangly, prehistoric bird. Painted a bright yellow, it sprouted spindly legs from a fat body. The tail was like an elongated ice cream cone with a small whirling propeller at the tip. The front end looked like the discarded greenhouse of a World War II trainer, and the whole cluster of disjointed parts dangled beneath a whirling, multiblade windmill.

As it labored tremulously toward us, the big blades on top beat the air with desperate ferocity, sending shock waves bouncing off the metal hangar, where I and the other incredulous pilots stood gaping. I saw it, but I didn't believe it. There were no wings! No aerodynamic surfaces! No stabilizers! It shouldn't fly. But it did, thrashing its way across the airfield a few feet above the ramp.

When it approached the group, a swirling blast of air smashed into the unsuspecting spectators, sending service caps—including the colonel's braided crown—sailing in all directions.

The Sikorsky model R-5A in which the author had his "First Flight" at McChord Field, Washington, summer 1947.

"Look at that crazy machine!" one of the pilots exclaimed. "I can't believe it!"

"I can't either," I muttered, watching with a strange fascination as the helicopter hovered in one spot for several minutes. Then it turned sideways, moved slowly out across the flight ramp, stopped, reversed itself, and moved back in the opposite direction, coming to a halt directly in front of us. Hovering there, it slowly turned around in a 360-degree circle, holding its position over the ramp. Then, as though saving its greatest feat until last, the helicopter, amazingly, began to move backward.

Watching the helicopter perform, I was struck with a disturbing ambivalence. It was homely and awkward-looking, without a single pleasing aerodynamic feature—an ugly duckling if I'd ever seen one. Yet it was uniquely graceful. There was something about the way it moved and the way it just hovered there, defying the laws of gravity and aerodynamics.

When the R-5 landed, it touched down as softly as a feather in front of our gawking group. After a moment or two, the engine sputtered and died, and all of the strange grinding noises began to subside as the long, fabric-covered rotor blades slowed, drooped down, and finally wobbled to a stop. A small door in the side of the nose section popped open, and a handsome second lieutenant with a Clark Gable mustache and a big smile climbed out. Facing this alien pilot, the colonel stood at the head of his army; his braided crown—which some brownnoser had retrieved—was pulled low, very low, over his eyes.

The helicopter pilot, wearing a bright red baseball cap with a gold bar pinned to the front, walked up to the colonel and flipped a smart salute. The colonel's only response was an ominous glare from his shadowed, squinting eyes. When it became evident to the helicopter pilot that he was not going to recieve the reception he expected, his smile faded.

"Is that special issue head gear for *heeleocopter* drivers?" the colonel snarled, glaring at the red cap.

The helicopter pilot nervously touched the bill of his cap. "Why, uh . . . yes. Yes, sir. We find that a ball cap is the most practical . . . uh, headgear for the helicopter. You see, colonel, we don't need an oxygen mask since the helicopter flies at low altitude and it . . ."

"On this military installation, lieutenant, you will wear regulation headgear. Is that clear?"

The helicopter pilot turned pale. "Yes . . . uh, yes, sir!" he blurted, snatching the cap from his head.

"Lieutenant, that was an interesting demonstration, but I don't anticipate we'll be needing a *heeleocopter* much around here. You can check with the line chief, and he'll see that it's stored in the hangar and out of the way of our other aircraft."

The helicopter pilot looked at the colonel incredulously. "But, sir . . . I was under the impression that . . ."

The colonel waved his hand for silence. "After you get it stored in the hangar, lieutenant, report to the headquarters orderly room with your orders."

"Yes, sir," said the helicopter pilot.

The colonel turned on his heel as some of the pilots and onlooking ground crew had begun to move toward the helicopter for a closer look. "That's it, gentlemen!" he snapped. "The formation is dismissed. You may return to your duty stations." Obediently, if not reluctantly, the curious ground crewmen dispersed and the pilots fell in behind the colonel, all marching off the flight ramp in order of rank, leaving the second lieutenant alone with his disdained helicopter.

As the procession exited the flight line, I discretely detached myself from the group and stepped, unseen, into the hangar through a side door. I then walked back through the interior and out onto the ramp.

I wasn't quite sure why, but, if for no other reason, I simply wanted to have a closer look at it. As I approached the helicopter, the pilot, with one hand still clutching the red ball cap, slowly raised his other hand to the side of his machine, as though in a gesture of defence.

I grinned at him and said confidentially, "Don't be misled by first impressions, lieutenant. You see, that colonel isn't really what he appears to be. Actually, he's a baboon we dress up to look like a colonel so we can test newcomers' compatibility with our little mishmash group here at McChord. Congratulations, I think you're in. I'm Richard Kirkland."

The helicopter pilot looked at me in round-eyed astonishment for a moment, then slowly accepted my handshake.

"Uh, yes, sir," he muttered. "I'm . . . uh, Walter Johnson."

"Glad to meet you, Walter. Just call me Kirk. Sorry about your reception, but if it's any consolation, I'm amazed at what you can do with this machine."

"I'm glad someone was impressed," groaned Johnson, shaking his head. "I can't believe that colonel."

"Yeah. He's a piece of work all right, but never mind him. Would you mind explaining to me how this flying machine works?"

It was evident by the expression on his face that the helicopter pilot was skeptical of my sincerity, so I added: "I'm serious, Walter. I'd really like to know how this bird manages to fly."

"You would?"

I nodded.

"Well . . . the basic aerodynamic principles are the same as on your airplane." Pausing, he glanced back over his shoulder, as though to insure the colonel had not returned. Then looking up at the rotor blades: "Those blades serve the same function as the wing on an airplane. The only difference being that your wing is attached to the fuselage, whereas my wing turns. And it turns for the same purpose: to create lift. Your wing is pulled through the air mass with an air screw . . . uh, propeller, to create lift and thus sustain flight. My wing is whirled thought the air mass, with the same result."

I glanced up at the rotor blades for a moment, then back at Johnson. It made sense. I had studied quite a bit of aerodynamic theory during training but, of course, nothing on rotary wing.

I nodded. "That makes sense."

Johnson smiled. "It sure does. There's nothing magic about it. Just plain ole aerodynamics, like any bird or airplane."

"But birds and airplanes all have tails for stability and directional control. How do you do it with a bird that doesn't have a tail?"

Some color had seeped back into Johnson's face, and his enthusiasm for the helicopter was beginning to show. "Oh, but it does have a tail: the tail rotor. See that little prop at the end of the tail cone?" He pointed toward the rear of the helicopter. "It does all the things for stability and directional control on the helicopter that your tail does on an airplane, and then some. You can change the angle of attack on that airfoil through application of the rudder pedals, thus countering engine torque, while providing directional control."

"Then the little prop in the back doesn't push?"

"No, it doesn't. The vertical, single-tail rotor on the helicopter is Igor Sikorsky's ingenious idea."

"I knew Sikorsky had designed some big four-engine flying boats, but I didn't realize he was this much into helicopters. Is this his first production model?"

"Oh, no. His first production model, the R-4, was produced for the Army during the war."

"They had helicopters in the Army Air Corps during the war?"

"Sure did."

"I never saw any."

"Well, they really only got a few into combat areas, and the R-4 was pretty limited. Now this one, the R-5, is quite an improvement." Johnson turned and looked at his helicopter admiringly. "This little baby has a lot more horsepower; she will really perform."

I stepped up and peeked into the cockpit. "There are some strange-looking levers in there. How do you control the attitude?"

"Here, let me show you," Johnson quickly offered, opening the side door. "The primary attitude is controlled with this lever here in the center of the cockpit. It's similar to the joystick on an airplane. We call it the azimuth, or cyclic control. Upon application, it changes the pitch on the main rotor blades . . . uh, pitch, meaning angle of attack."

"I understand."

"Anyway, it changes the pitch selectively during the cycle of rotation, which in turn tips the rotor plane in whatever direction you've selected. It's sort of like on an airplane. When you push forward, the nose goes down; pull back, and the nose comes up."

"Okay, I follow that. But how do you go straight up? How do you hover?"

"Good question," Johnson said, obviously pleased at my interest. He reached across the cockpit and grasped another lever. "This is called the collective-pitch stick, and, when you move it up or down, it changes the angle of attack on all of the rotor blades simultaneously. See?"

"I thought you said the azimuth stick changed the angle of attack?"

"Well, it does, but selectively for directional movement. This stick does it collectively for ascent or descent."

"Wait a minute. You just ran out of hands. If you got one hand on that stick, the . . . uh, collective, and the other on the cyclic, and your feet on the rudders, how are you gonna work the throttle?"

"That's easy," Johnson replied. "It's another of Mr. Sikorsky's innovations. There is a motorcycle-type twist throttle on the collective stick. Look here. See how it twists?"

I gave a low whistle. "You gotta be busier than a one-armed paperhanger to fly this thing."

"Well, yeah. . . . You're busy all right. But it's not all that bad once you get the hang of it."

I stepped back and shook my head. "That's some kind of a machine. How did you ever happen to get stuck flying these things?"

"Well, I joined the Army Air Corps to be a fighter pilot and somehow I ended up in helicopters. But you know how it goes in the good ole Army."

I laughed. "Yeah, I know how it goes in the good ole Army. But your first choice was good anyway. I don't know about this one."

"Well, I'll tell ya, lieutenant . . . uh, Kirk. I wanted to be a fighter pilot all right, but now I wouldn't trade you places for all the tea in China. I love it, and I'll tell you something else: this machine, the helicopter, will someday play a major roll in aviation."

"Think so, huh?"

"Absolutely. Did you know the basic idea of vertical flight was conceived by Leonardo da Vinci, way back in the fifteenth century?"

"Nope."

"Yeah. The word helicopter comes from the Greek words *heliko,* meaning spiral, and *pteron,* meaning wing. Thus: spiral wing."

"Interesting."

"Although I guess you'd say we are still in first-generation technology, there have been some significant advances in just a few short years."

"There have?"

"Yeah. Despite the general impression that it's just a novelty with no real mission, I can tell you it has some remarkable capabilities."

"It has, huh?"

"Yeah. I wish I could show you."

"Well, why not?" I said, grinning.

The color drained from Johnson's face as a vision of the snarling colonel flashed before his eyes. "Ah . . . well, you know, the colonel?"

"Well, the baboon colonel said to store it, and getting it ready for storage could include a test hop to adjust the . . . ah, azimuth?"

As the helicopter pilot stood looking at me curiously, the line chief and two of his crew appeared. "Sir, I've been ordered to put this, uh, machine into hangar storage," the sergeant said courteously.

Johnson glanced at the sergeant, then at me. "Well."

"Didn't you determine, Lieutenant Johnson, that this bird requires a test hop?" I asked in an authoritative voice.

"Why . . . uh . . . yes, sir. I should make one . . . test flight, before we put the R-5 into storage."

The two crewmen accompanying the line chief looked at the sergeant, who glanced up at the yellow helicopter, then back to the lieutenant with an expression that read: Don't try to con me, shavetail. But the wily sergeant tempered his response with, "Sir, the colonel was quite explicit in his orders. I was told to—"

"This aircraft's gotta have a test hop, sarge," I interrupted. "He has to make some azimuth adjustments to prevent damage to the . . . uh, torque bearings while she's in storage. Isn't that right, lieutenant?"

The helicopter pilot gave me a surprised look, then nodded.

"Besides, I'll assume responsibility, since I'm going with the lieutenant," I added.

The senior master sergeant was an old-timer who had dealt with many a smart-ass officer, and he was not easily intimidated. But he knew I was no prima donna, so, glancing at his wristwatch, he said, "Very well, Lieutenant Kirkland. How long will you be, sir? You know, it's Friday afternoon."

"We won't be long," interjected Johnson, opening the door to the front cockpit and motioning to me.

I started to climb in, then noticed there was no parachute in the seat. "Uh, lieutenant, there's no chute up here; I'll have to run and get one."

"Another of the great features of the helicopter, sir. No parachute necessary."

I stared at Johnson incredulously. I'd never flown without a parachute. And, as far as I knew, regulations required they be worn in all Army aircraft.

"I'm serious," assured Johnson. "Here, look in my seat. See, no parachute." I glanced into the backseat. Indeed there was no parachute.

"What about regulations?"

"Not required in the helicopter."

"Well, what if it shoots craps?"

"If we have a problem . . . uh, shoots craps, we simply land. And we can land anywhere: on a road, in a backyard, in a pea patch. Wherever. The helicopter doesn't need a runway to land on; it takes its own landing field right with it."

I was skeptical. "What happens to the windmill if the motor stops?" I asked, jabbing my thumb upward at the rotor blades.

"If the engine quits, we just windmill down," he explained confidently. "We call it 'autorotation.' It's just as good as a parachute."

I glanced at the line chief, who stood a short distance away with his arms folded across his chest, the hint of a smile on his face. I climbed into the helicopter and strapped myself in tight, while a little voice in my head asked: "What are you doing, Kirkland?"

"Clear!" shouted Johnson from the rear cockpit a moment later.

The cranking noise of the starter reminded me of a model A Ford I had once owned. Finally, the engine coughed, belched a cloud of black smoke, and roared to life.

After a short warm-up, the engine began to labor and the three long rotor blades started to move. As their revolutions increased they began to rise, increasing speed until their resolution was a blur above the helicopter. Simultaneously, the sounds and vibrations of many laboring dynamics filled the cockpit. I had been around flying machines long enough to recognize that there were a multitude of torque bearings in this bird all right, so I had not been totally fibbing to the line chief.

I heard Johnson call the tower for takeoff clearance and then over the intercom to me: "Now I'm going to increase the angle of attack on the main rotor blades by pulling up on the collective-pitch stick, and that will cause the helicopter to lift vertical. We call it 'pulling pitch.'"

Without acceleration of speed or sound, the whirling, tremulous machine simply lifted itself up off the earth, and I realized instantly that a new dimension was to be added to my fascination for flying—the third dimension: vertical flight!

There was, as my troubled instincts had suggested, a freedom of movement, a thrilling release from the surly bonds of earth, that was even more sensational and thrilling than conventional flight. And I couldn't help wonder, in a passing thought, how John Gillespie Magee might have worded the poem "High Flight" if he could have flown a helicopter?

I was vaguely aware that Johnson was explaining control movements, but my attention was focused on the esoteric sensations I was experiencing as the helicopter moved over its omnidirectional course. What a strange contrast in sight and sound to that which I was so familiar. Absent was the headlong rush for takeoff and the rising crescendo of engine noise and wind roar over the canopy. The helicopter had just lifted itself up into the airspace, defying gravity and moving with boundless freedom. Similar to the way a hummingbird can fly.

"If I push one of the rudder pedals, the helicopter will turn in that direction, and if I hold it, the helicopter will go around in a circle, see?" said Johnson, and it did. "Now, if I want to go forward, I ease the cyclic stick forward and presto!" We began to move forward. "And unlike an airplane, I can fly backward by simply moving the cyclic stick aft." Sure enough, we began to fly backward.

After a moment we stopped. "Now we'll do what's called hover flying, which is maneuvering around near the ground at slow speeds in what is called 'ground effect.'" We began to move sideways across the flight ramp, past the line of hangars. Then, coming to a stop, Johnson applied rudder pedal, swinging the tail around to where the nose had been. Now we began to move forward again, slowly, across the grass beyond the runways and over a small creek that ran along the perimeter of the airfield. I glanced down into the clear water and saw a rainbow trout dash under a rock. I had wondered if there were any fish in that creek. Now I knew; there was at least one.

When we reached the edge of the tree line, Johnson said, "Time for takeoff, and we don't need a runway. I just point the nose into the wind and pull pitch in conjunction with a little forward cyclic. The helicopter then transitions from 'ground effect,' known as 'translational lift,' into forward flight. Now we fly like an airplane."

As Johnson increased his pull on the collective-pitch lever, the helicopter lifted up and over the tall evergreens, its landing wheels skimming along the top branches. As we passed over the village that bordered the air base, a woman in a bright orange dress looked up from hanging clothes in her backyard. I plainly saw the surprised look on her face. How clearly and easily I could see detail that would only be a fleeting blur from an airplane. Then my eye caught another movement below: a covey of quail fluttered into a thicket, and a cottontail rabbit dashed in the opposite direction. It was as though I was suspended on a moving skyhook that featured a grand, panoramic view of the passing parade of life below.

Suddenly I sensed the helicopter was slowing. An instinctive warning went off in my brain: approaching stall speed. Watch it! But we didn't stall. The helicopter gave a little extra shudder and came to a stop in midair, where it hovered, above the treetops, in one cubicle of airspace. "Try this in your ole fighter plane!" I heard Johnson say over the intercom. "It's called 'hovering out of ground effect.'"

Then the helicopter began to sink down through an opening between the treetops. I could see branches waving and dancing all around me from the wind of the rotor blades. I grabbed onto the interior structure of the cockpit in anticipation of an imminent crash. But the helicopter's descent gradually slowed and stopped as it came to a hover. Then the wheels gently settled into a carpet of thick, green grass on the bank of a picturesque brook nestled in a grove of evergreens.

When we landed back on the flight ramp at McChord Army Air Forces Base a short time later and all the machinery had ground to a stop, I crawled out of the front cockpit and stood silently staring at the Sikorsky R-5 while ambivalent thoughts ricocheted inside my head. Flying was the love of my life. And the ultimate in flying was an agile, swift, fighter plane. I knew that; everyone knew that. So what was this? How did this strange machine fit into the picture? It was ugly. It was noisy. It was tremulous. Yet it was fascinating: the freedom of movement, the sensation of vertical ascent and descent, the hovering in midair, and the landing in a meadow. . . .

"Isn't that some way to fly?" asked Johnson.

I looked into the helicopter pilot's beaming face. "Yeah, it sure is," I muttered. "It was some kind of experience all right." Then, as though to myself: "But it was . . . very disturbing."

"Why do you say it was disturbing?" Johnson's smile was now tempered with curiosity.

I glanced back at the helicopter, as though it might answer my question, because I didn't have an answer. All I knew was that I'd just had an experience that left me exhilarated, yet confused and strangely anxious.

"Lieutenant Kirkland," interrupted the line chief, walking up next to the helicopter. "The colonel wants you to report to his office immediately."

I pulled my eyes from the helicopter and looked at the sergeant accusingly. "Sarge, did you squeal on me?"

"No, sir!" replied the sergeant, shaking his head. "Wasn't me, Lieutenant Kirkland. Honest Injun."

As I stepped into the headquarters orderly room, the wormy little captain, who was the colonel's adjutant, looked at me with a smirk on his face, and I knew I was in trouble. Sure enough, a few minutes later when I stood at attention on the carpet in front of the colonel's desk, his opening salvo was: "Who the hell do you think you are, Kirkland?"

"Well . . . uh . . ."

"Shut up!"

"Yes, sir."

"You think just because you got a couple of hero badges in the war you can get away with whatever you want, don't you?"

"No, sir, I . . ."

"Let me tell you something, lieutenant. In case you didn't know it, the war is over. The days of you fighter jocks cutting a wide swath is over, too. We are back to the regular Army days and back to proper discipline. Do you understand me, lieutenant?"

"Yes, sir."

"I ordered that contraption hangared, and that didn't exempt the great you."

"I . . ."

"Shut up!"

As the colonel stared at me silently for a moment, I could tell from the look on his face that the wheels in his fat head were grinding away. Sure enough, a little smile eased out, and he leaned back in his chair.

"You know I think I just came up with the perfect solution for a smart-ass like you, Kirkland. You and that piece of junk were made for each other. We just received a requisition for a pilot to go to *heeleocopter* school. Guess who I'm going to volunteer for that slot?"

And, so it was that day long ago that I stood in front of the colonel with conflicting emotions churning within me. I had an awful feeling that my dream of flying jet fighters was up in smoke. Yet there was a vibrant new excitement at the thought of flying that fascinating machine: the helicopter!

I was sent to the USAF Helicopter Pilot School in Waco, Texas, where I began a love affair that remains as passionate today as it was a half century ago.

I may have exaggerated a little about the colonel's dislike for helicopters, but not much. There was some curiosity in those early days, but limited genuine interest by the military or the general aviation world, who considered the helicopter a novelty with limited capabilities and little future. In 1909 Wilbur Wright wrote:

> *Like all novices we began with the helicopter (in childhood) but soon saw that it had no future and dropped it. The helicopter does with great labor only what the balloon does without labor, and is no more fitted than the balloon for rapid horizontal flight. If its engine stops it must fall with deathly violence for it can neither float like the balloon nor glide like the aeroplane. The helicopter is much easier to design than the aeroplane but it is worthless when done.*

But then nobody's perfect, and Wilbur didn't know about autorotation in 1909. A little later on there were some who saw it differently, like Igor Sikorsky, Frank Piasecki, Larry Bell, Stanley Hiller, and Charlie Kaman.

2

Chopper Down

The tall, lanky pilot sitting on his GI cot in a GI pyramidal tent fished a cigarette out of his shirt pocket and stuck it between his lips. As he fired it with a Zippo lighter, a field phone hanging on one end of his cot screeched. He reached across his bed and pulled the phone from its canvas case.

"Panmunjom, Lieutenant DuPont," he said with puffs of smoke tumbling out.

"This is Captain Durbin at JOC [Joint Operations Control]. We got a pilot down, and we're trying to locate a chopper to go get him. You got one available?"

DuPont frowned. "This is special operations at Panmunjom, Captain. You need to call rescue control at K-16."

"I've already called them, and they don't have a chopper available that could get up there in time."

"Well, we got one. But as you know, it's on special duty for the VIPs at the peace talks in Kaesong."

"This is an operational emergency, lieutenant. We got a pilot down in enemy territory, and that chopper is the only one that can possibly get to him before dark."

It was fall 1951, and the United Nations had been fighting a "police action" war in Korea since September 1950. Although peace talks were ongoing, little had changed in the vicious fighting. Lt. Charles J. Dupont, a U.S. Air Force helicopter pilot, stood mute for a moment, holding the phone in one hand and a burning cigarette in the other.

"Lieutenant?"

"Yeah. . . . Where is he, Capt'n?"

"He's down in sector 14 Zebra."

He knew where 14 Zebra was: not all that far in a fighter plane, but a long damn way into enemy territory for a slow-moving chopper. "Okay. Capt'n, we'll go get 'em."

"Great. Have the pilot call us on the emergency frequency as soon as he's airborne, and we'll give him details and CAP [combat air patrol] information."

DuPont nodded, dropped the phone back into its case, and took a last puff of his cigarette before grinding it out. He lifted his survival vest and .45 pistol belt from where it hung on a two-by-four tent railing and started out through the door when the field phone screeched again. He turned and picked it up. "DuPont here."

"Charlie, this is Bob. What's goin' on?"

Capt. Bob Barnhill was the operations officer of Detachment F of the 3rd Air Rescue Squadron at K-16, Seoul, Korea, to which DuPont was assigned.

"I just told JOC that we'd send our VIP chopper to pick up the downed pilot."

"Have you cleared it with the general?"

"No. He's not here."

Hesitation.

"Bob, this chopper has to go now if we're gonna pick up that pilot before dark."

"Yeah, you're right. Who's flying the mission?"

"Yours truly, and I gotta get going."

"What? You can't do that, Charlie. You're grounded from combat flying. Get somebody else to fly the mission."

"There ain't anybody else, Bob. I'm the only one here. The other pilots are up at Kaesong at the peace conference. I either go pick up that pilot or he's in deep kimchee. As soon as it's dark his CAP will have to leave, and the commies will grab him . . . or kill him. One is as bad as the other."

"I know, but . . . Jesus, Charlie, you've flown your ninety missions and that's gonna be a rough one; 14 Zebra is in a heavy concentration of North Korean troops."

"Well, I sure as hell don't like hearing that, Bob. But it doesn't change anything. I gotta go try to get him. There isn't any other option, is there?"

Hesitation. "No . . . no, I guess not. We don't have another chopper available that could get up there in time . . . I guess you drew the short straw, ole friend."

"Yeah. So it goes, Bob."

Charlie had picked up wounded GIs off the battlefield and snatched downed air crew from the Yellow Sea and behind enemy lines ninety times in a slow, unarmed, and totally unprotected helicopter. The Korean War chopper had not been designed for combat and was therefore highly vulnerable. But life saving on the battlefield had been Charlie's job, and he had done it. When he finished his missions, however, he knew that he had stretched his luck to the limit, and it was time to go home.

About that time, the North Koreans had agreed to hold peace talks (while the war continued to rage), and the colonel had talked him into extending his tour of duty because they needed chopper pilots to fly the United Nations delegates from Panmunjom, South Korea, to Kaesong, North Korea. Since ninety was the maximum missions a pilot was allowed to fly, he would no longer be flying combat missions, but would be performing a great service for his country and the United Nations—so the colonel said.

DuPont walked out of his tent across to the one next door and stuck his head in. "I need a volunteer for a pilot pickup in North Korea."

Medical technician Sgt. Joe Fryer, sitting on a wooden box sewing a hole in his sock, looked at DuPont, then glanced around the empty tent and grinned. "By process of elimination, I guess that means me, lieutenant."

"You'll do. And hustle it up, Joe."

"How come you're flying a combat mission, Lieutenant DuPont? I thought you were grounded."

"Yeah, so did I."

A few minutes later, with Joe Fryer, his medical kit, and his .30 caliber carbine in the rear seat of the Sikorsky H-5 helicopter, DuPont pulled pitch and headed toward Inchon, on the west coast of Korea.

"JOC, this is Pedro Zero Nine [Air Force rescue helicopter call sign]. I'm airborne," he transmitted on the emergency VHF [very high frequency] radio.

"Roger, Pedro Zero Nine is airborne. We have confirmed that 14 Zebra is the grid location of the downed pilot. He is from the 51st Fighter Interceptor Wing, and he's being CAP'ed by F-80s from his squadron, call sign 'Hammer.' The call sign of your CAP is 'Grenadier Love.' They're a South African flight of four F-51s, and they should be up on 121.5 shortly" [121.5 was the emergency radio frequency].

"Roger, JOC."

That's one bit of good news, thought Charlie. He had been capped before by the South Africans and they were good, and the F-51 was an excellent CAP aircraft. It could get down where the jets couldn't.

"Pedro Zero Nine, for rendezvous with your CAP, what's gonna be your ingress position and altitude?"

"I'd like to rendezvous with Grenadier Love over Inchon at 5,000 feet, JOC."

"Okay, I'll so advise them."

Charlie would have preferred to go in on the treetops, because at 5,000 feet in a chopper you were a perfect target for antiaircraft fire. But then at low altitude you took small-arms fire—or so the rationale went that established the 5,000-foot policy.

To minimize exposure, his plan was to fly west until he was directly south of 14 Zebra, which was near Inchon, pick up his CAP, and then turn north. If the pilot's location was correct, he would have to fly about forty miles inside North Korea—a long time to be exposed to enemy fire. But the South Africans would be merciless toward whomever shot at him—and each fighter packed deadly firepower.

"Pedro Zero Nine, this is Grenadier Love, we have you in sight," came the radio call as DuPont approached Inchon.

"Roger, Grenadier Love, I have you in sight also, and I'm making my turn north," replied Charlie as he spotted the formation of four F-51s arching across the sky above him.

"Roger, ole chap, let us know if you take any fire."

"You'll hear me loud and clear, Grenadier Love. Request you send one of your birds on up to 14 Zebra and give me a report on conditions."

"Roger. Number Four, pop on up there and take a look."

"Righto, lead. Number Four breaking off."

Lieutenant Dupont watched one of the P-51s peel off and accelerate to the north as the remaining three circled above the slow-flying helicopter.

As he flew northward at 5,000 feet, Dupont could see the vast Inchon tidelands, dotted with islands, stretching westward to the Yellow Sea. To the north, an overcast blocked the late-afternoon sun and cast a dull gray over the mountainous area ahead, as though a harbinger of what lie ahead.

"Grenadier Love lead, this is Four; go to tach frequency."

"Negative! Negative!" barked Charlie on the radio. "I'm the one that's gotta go in there, so I want to hear what's going on!"

"Roger, ole chap, we'll stay on this frequency. What's the story, Four?"

"Not too good," replied the pilot of Grenadier Love Four. "The downed pilot is hiding in a graveyard. But the place is swarming with North Korean troops. They do have a CAP of eight F-80s up there, and they're tearing up the countryside, but there's troops all over the place."

"He's hiding in a graveyard?"

"Yeah, he's on a hill in the graveyard, and the gooks are all around it."

Damn! That meant ground fire when he went in to make the pickup. It was going to be a rough mission all right, Charlie said to himself.

"Pedro Zero Nine, did you receive that information?"

"Yeah. I'd rather not have, but I got it, Grenadier Love."

"More bad news, ole chap," transmitted Number Four. "There's weather moving in. You can see the storm front over the mountains to the north, and I'd guess it will be over that area within the next half hour or so."

"Super," DuPont grumbled. Checking his map against the landmarks below, it appeared he had about fifteen miles to go, which should put him there before the bad weather struck. But that was probably the least of his worries. The only good news so far was that he had taken no antiaircraft fire.

Turning around in his seat, he shouted, "Keep an eye out for antiaircraft fire, Joe!" Since this vintage chopper did not have an intercom, communications depended on good ole shouting.

The medic scooted forward in the backseat and shouted back, "Okay, lieutenant! Is this gonna be a hot one?"

"I'm afraid it is, Joe!"

Fryer nodded and moved back into his seat. Charlie felt sympathy for the poor medic who could do nothing but sit back there and hope for the best. At least he, as the pilot, could feel that he had some control over his own destiny . . . or did he?

"Pedro Zero Nine, this is Hammer. You read?" came a new transmission in Dupont's earphones.

"Roger, Hammer, Pedro Zero Nine here."

"We're the CAP on station, Pedro, what's your ETA?"

"About ten minutes, Hammer. How does it look?"

"Our guy is okay for now, but you're gonna be just in time. The valley is swarming with troops. We've kept them off the mountain where he is, but a few may have slipped through, so we need to get him out of there—the sooner the better."

"Okay, Hammer, how is the weather?"

"Not good. It's moving in fast. But we'll be able to work the area over once more before you get here."

As he approached the area of 14 Zebra, about ten minutes later, Charlie could see mushrooming clouds of black smoke caused by the attacking flight of jets that were strafing and firing rockets into the North Korean troop installations. He could also see the dark weather clouds moving down from the north.

"Hammer, this is Pedro Zero Nine. I'm over the south end of the valley now with my CAP, Grenadier Love. I'll be in position in a couple minutes to go in for the pickup," transmitted DuPont.

"Roger, I got you spotted. Hammer flight from lead, break off. Repeat, break off, the chopper is here and starting his run. Pedro Zero Nine, you got the graveyard in sight?"

After a short eye search, Charlie spotted the mountaintop graveyard. "Okay, Hammer and Grenadier Love, I got the graveyard in sight, and I plan to make my approach to the north."

"Sound off if you take any fire, Pedro," responded the Grenadier Love leader.

"You'll be the first to hear about it, Grenadier Love."

"Joe, keep a sharp lookout for ground fire!" he shouted to the back and lowered the collective, nosing the helicopter downward.

As he flew down over the valley, DuPont saw the mountain ahead with the graveyard on top, and suddenly he remembered that Koreans bury their dead straight up. The graveyard was covered with mounds. He wouldn't be able to land, and the helicopter he was flying did not have a personnel hoist. What else could go wrong?

"Joe, we're going in for the pickup. Don't open the cabin door till I tell you!"

"Yes, sir! Are you gonna try to land?"

"Can't land because of the grave mounds! I'll come to a hover, and you signal the pilot to grab onto the helicopter, then try to pull him inside!"

"Okay, but I don't see him!"

"Neither do I!"

"Maybe the gooks got him!"

It would be a hell of a note if the pilot had been captured at this point, thought Charlie as he eased in aft cyclic and lowered pitch to set up his approach to the mountaintop.

"You getting any ground fire, Pedro Zero Nine?" asked Grenadier Love from the cockpit of his F-51, as the four South African fighters circled over the small valley with the eight F-80s.

"So far it's negative on ground fire, Grenadier Love. But I can't see the pilot. Where is he?"

"There he is, lieutenant!" Fryer shouted suddenly, leaning forward from the backseat and pointing a finger.

Charlie saw a figure run out from behind a grave mound, waving his arms frantically. "I got him," he said, banking slightly and pulling pitch to establish a hover. But as the H-5 settled toward the graveyard, he realized that the swirling winds from the approaching storm had shifted, causing the helicopter to yaw and buck violently.

He pulled pitch, nosed off to one side, and kicked rudder pedal to bring the helicopter back around for another approach. He could see the pilot chasing after him through the grave mounds, apparently afraid they were leaving without him.

"Open the cabin door!" Charlie shouted. "When I come to a hover over the mounds, he's gonna have to grab on!"

"Lieutenant! There's soldiers with guns right below us!" yelled the medic.

Charlie saw the North Korean soldiers in his peripheral vision, but his concentration focused on bringing the helicopter into a hover that would allow the pilot to climb in. But if he went too low, the tail rotor would strike one of the burial mounds, and that would be all she wrote.

He glanced out and saw the pilot, who was racing toward the helicopter, suddenly stop, raise his arm, and fire his .45 at two soldiers who were chasing him. Then he turned and ran toward the helicopter that was yawing and pitching in the shifting winds.

The pilot ran up to the helicopter and made a desperate lunge for the open door. Joe Fryer, hanging out of the door, grabbed him and hung on. All DuPont could hope was that Fryer had a good grip on the pilot, because soldiers had suddenly appeared directly in front of the helicopter. It was either pull pitch now or take a head-on fusillade of North Korean lead.

Charlie cranked the throttle full open and pulled all the pitch he could get.

"Pedro Zero Nine from Hammer, did you get 'em?"

No answer.

"Hammer to Pedro Zero Nine! Did you get Vern?"

DuPont heard Hammer's plea of concern for their squadron mate, but his total concentration was on flying the helicopter as fast as it would go away from the ground fire that he knew was pouring into the H-5.

He glanced back. The pilot was still hanging onto the side of the helicopter, with Fryer struggling to pull him inside.

"Answer me, chopper!" came the angry voice of Hammer.

"I don't know yet," said Charlie.

"What?"

"I got 'em in, lieutenant!" shouted Fryer from behind.

Charlie DuPont felt that sudden, acute feeling of relief that he had always felt after snatching someone from the enemy's grasp. "We got him, Hammer," he said calmly over the radio.

"Hey! That's great! Everybody hear that? The chopper got Vern!"

Cheers were heard on radio frequency 121.5 as the CAP pilots looked down and saw the flashing blades of the Sikorsky helicopter skimming out across the mountain ridges of North Korea.

In the cabin of the helicopter, Fryer leaned forward, tapped DuPont on the back, and shouted, "Lieutenant, the pilot says that when he jumped onto the chopper he saw oil streaming out of the engine! He's got it all over him!"

Lady luck giveth and she taketh away, thought Charlie DuPont as he glanced at the oil-pressure gage and saw the needle pegged on zero.

"Grenadier Love, this is Pedro Zero Nine. I got trouble."

"What's the problem, Pedro Zero Nine?"

"I took ground fire, and I got no engine oil pressure."

Silence.

"What are your intentions, ole chap?"

Yeah, DuPont . . . what are you gonna do?

"Stand by, Grenadier Love."

"Roger."

You can't will that Pratt & Whitney to keep running without oil. How long will it run? Not long. . . . You're going to have to land down there, and it's too late in the day to get choppers up here to get the three of you out. . . . The commies will be coming when they see you go down. . . . And the CAP can't protect you at night—they will have to go on home. . . . You should have known your luck couldn't last forever. . . .

DuPont glanced down at the terrain below. The canyons were already turning a dark blue gray as nightfall approached and the storm clouds moved relentlessly over the ridges. Not many places down there to make an autorotation landing. . . . But that's what he had to do. The engine can't run without oil, and, barring divine intervention, the helicopter was going down when it quit. . . . Maybe he could make it to the coast before it quit? . . . It wasn't too far, was it?

"Grenadier Love, I'm gonna try to make it to the coast. Call JOC and have them launch an SA-16 [twin-engine amphibian aircraft]. If I can make it, they can pick us up over there."

"Roger, wilco."

"Pedro Zero Nine, this is Hammer. We're low on fuel, but we'll help cover you as long as we can."

"Roger, Hammer."

Charlie turned his head and shouted, "Joe, buckle yourselves in tight! We got a rough landing comin' up!"

When he turned back to the instrument panel, he saw the cylinder head temperature gauge had pegged in the red. The radio became silent now as the CAP F-51 and F-80 fighters circled above the OD-colored [olive drab] helicopter flying over the darkening mountains.

"Grenadier Love from Pedro Zero Nine. Can you see how far it is to the coast?"

"Yeah. I can see the coastline. It's not too far after you cross that next ridge."

Directly ahead was a heavily wooded ridge. If the engine quit while flying over it he would have to autorotate into the trees—not good. Somebody would get hurt for sure. Directly ahead, just before the ridge, was a small plateau of rice paddies. He could land there all right, . . . but they were North Korean rice paddies. If he could just make it over that ridge. . . . Come on, baby, you can run just a little longer, can't you?

Oil pressure zero, cylinder-head temperature gauge pegged, and an engine making strange noises. It was decision time. Charlie eased off on the collective and back on the cyclic for an approach to the rice paddies directly ahead. "Grenadier Love, I'm gonna have to land in the rice paddies up ahead. Let me know if you see any activity."

"Pedro Zero Nine, you're not all that far from the coast, and JOC has an SA-16 and a chopper en route to the area."

"I've got a feeling that I can't make it over that ridge, Grenadier Love."

Charlie had discovered in his first ninety combat missions that when he got that certain feeling, he should act on it. And it was well that he did. As he brought the helicopter up over the rice paddies, the engine gave out a groan and quit dead.

His instinct was correct, but he was just a few yards short of the rice paddy and had to make his landing on the lip of the paddy, which caused the H-5 to topple over on its side. The rotor blades struck the ground, and the helicopter thrashed around violently until the blades had beat themselves to death, hurling pieces all over the countryside.

When the thrashing subsided and all the pieces came to rest, the three men scrambled out of the wreckage, fortunately uninjured. They stood for a moment, staring at the twisted and broken helicopter. They had lost their means of escape, but somehow they knew the Sikorsky helicopter had given its all.

"She did pretty well, considering," muttered Charlie, noticing all the bullet holes in the engine compartment.

"Yeah, and it got me out of that graveyard," added Lt. Vernon Wright, the jet pilot.

DuPont glanced around the plateau of rice paddies. "I don't see any activity, but you fellows keep a sharp watch while I get out my URC-4" [utility radio communications].

"You got one of those?" asked Wright.

"Yeah, I'm lucky to have it. They're new and there's precious few of them around. I just hope it works," said Charlie, fishing the small, handheld emergency radio out of his survival jacket. "Come on, baby, work," he mumbled, pulling up the antenna and switching it on. "Grenadier Love, this is Pedro ground, do you read?"

No answer. Then: "Who is calling Grenadier Love?"

"It's me! Pedro . . . I'm on the ground with a URC-4 radio."

"I say, ole chap, what a pleasant surprise, and I can read you five square," came the response.

DuPont knew at that instant the playing field had been leveled again. With ground-to-air communications, and a little luck, they could still get out of this alive. (This is believed to have been the first emergency use of the URC-4 radio in the Korean War. It subsequently became required survival equipment for air crews and was responsible for saving many a downed airman.)

"Pedro, are you okay down there? Your helicopter looks done in."

"Roger, Grenadier Love. But no one was hurt. What's the status of the rescue chopper?"

"JOC just called and said it had to turn back because of weather and darkness. I'm afraid you chaps are gonna have to spend the night there." That vintage helicopter had no lights or instruments for night flying.

The first report coming through the URC-4 was not good news for the stranded airmen. "That doesn't thrill us," groaned DuPont.

"But JOC is launching two choppers at dawn, weather permitting," added Grenadier Love.

"Yeah . . . weather permitting," Charlie muttered, as the cold wind of the season's first winter storm whipped his clothing.

"Okay. Do you see any military activity around us?"

"We can't see any activity in your immediate area. There is some kind of military installation a couple miles north of you, and we spotted what looked like troops moving out. You might want to get out of that area rather quickly."

"Okay. Grenadier Love, we're gonna do just that."

"Roger, Pedro. You can count on our being back up here at the crack of dawn . . . weather permitting."

"Thanks. Look for us south of here. When I see you overhead, I'll contact you on the URC-4. And, uh . . . Grenadier Love, if it doesn't work out, we want you to know we appreciate your efforts."

"Pedro, all the pilots and crews in Korea know the great work you chaps do, so you can count on us doing everything we can to get you out of there. Good luck, and we'll see you in the morning," said the Grenadier Love leader, who then winged over with his flight of F-51 fighters and swooped down over the three figures standing beside the wrecked helicopter. When the sound of the Rolls-Royce engines in the F-51s had faded, it was replaced by the howl of a winter wind sweeping across the hulk of the fallen chopper.

"We're in for a rough night, fellows, no matter what we do. But I think we better get on out of here before some of our North Korean friends show up," said Charlie, glancing up at the ridge. "I suggest we climb about halfway up the side of that ridge, then head south. I've got a magnetic compass with a luminous dial to keep our direction."

"Why halfway up, lieutenant?" asked Fryer.

"Well, I'd bet that North Korean GIs are no different than any other GIs, so they will do what is the easiest, which is to search the valleys and the tops of the ridges."

Vernon nodded. "Sounds reasonable to me. What's the plan if we do encounter soldiers?"

The three looked at each other. DuPont and Wright wore regulation .45-caliber service pistols. Fryer held a regulation .30-caliber carbine. "I suggest we let the decision to fight or surrender depend on the situation," offered Charlie. The others nodded.

The three men forged their way through the woods until they were about halfway up the side of the ridge. Then DuPont took a bearing with his magnetic compass, and they headed south.

Darkness had settled now, which made traversing the forest a stumbling, falling, cursing exercise, exacerbated by a howling wind and a brutal downpour of freezing rain. The winter storm had struck with a fury, and within a short time all three were soaked to the skin, and numbed by the freezing temperatures. They forged on, stopping occasionally to rest for only a few minutes.

"It's colder than a well digger's ass in the Klondike," groaned the medic as they halted for a rest after several hours of trudging doggedly through the freezing rain.

"I'm so cold I can't feel a thing," put in Wright. "You suppose we're freezing to death?"

"They taught us in medical training that just before you freeze to death, you feel warm and comfortable," said Fryer.

"Well, then I'm not freezing to death," growled DuPont. "Because I'm one cold, miserable, son of a bitch!"

That touch of humor spurred them on through the dark forest. They tried to move as quietly as possible, but were unable to suppress the noise of cracking brush and tree limbs, and an occasional outburst of cursing when someone fell or got a twig jabbed in his eye.

At one point Fryer stepped off a twenty-foot cliff and bruised his hip badly. "Maybe we should stop and try to find some kind of shelter," suggested Wright.

"The only shelter we're likely to find if we don't keep going is a North Korean prison," Charlie replied. "If Joe can walk, we've got to keep going."

"Yeah, I'll make it, lieutenant. I'd rather freeze to death than end up in a gook prison camp."

The jet pilot, with freezing water dripping off his nose, nodded agreement, and they wordlessly moved out behind DuPont, who had assumed the role of leader.

Sometime in the early morning hours the temperature dropped well below freezing, but the wind and rain slacked off and occasionally the moon peeked through the clouds. The moonlight was a morale booster but made traveling more treacherous, since one moment they would be in bright moonlight and the next, pitch blackness.

At one point they stopped to rest and suddenly heard voices coming through the woods. They grabbed their firearms and dove for cover behind a clump of trees. They remained motionless, hardly daring to breathe for some time. Was it soldiers, or villagers? They never found out, since whoever it was went off in the opposite direction.

After that tense experience, they struggled on until shortly before dawn, when Fryer could not continue on his injured hip. Charlie had wanted to get to an open place in the forest, where the CAP could see them the next morning, but he realized that all three of them were exhausted and had gone as far as they could go. He would have to rely on the URC-4. If it worked like it had earlier, the CAP could find them, and the rescue choppers could be directed in to pick them up. If it didn't work . . . sayonara.

They didn't dare build a fire, so all they could do was huddle in the wet brush and count the minutes till dawn. Without movement, the terrible cold was now a real threat to their survival. Charlie recognized the dangers of stopping, and he had pushed them to the limit. But now there was nothing to do but hope the rescue aircraft would arrive early as promised.

When the first streaks of dawn broke across the North Korean ridges, Charlie checked off one of his worries. The storm had passed, and the sky was going to be clear. That meant the rescue aircraft would come. He reached into his survival vest for the radio, but his hands were so cold he couldn't grasp it. Then came a terrifying thought. Would the URC-4 even work in this bitter cold?

He climbed to his feet and began to beat his hands together to get some feeling. His cigarettes had turned to rain-soaked mush early in the night, but his old-fashioned Zippo lighter flamed when he flicked the little start wheel. He held his hand over the fire until he smelt flesh burning. Then he heard the distinct sound of an F-51.

"They're here! They're here!" he croaked.

As promised, a flight of four South African F-51s streaked across the early morning sky as DuPont frantically tried to get the antenna up and the radio turned on. It was difficult to tell if he had actually pushed the switch on with his frozen hands. He waited. The F-51s passed over and continued on. They would have gone by, of course, because they couldn't see him in the trees.

"Grenadier Love! Grenadier Love! You passed us!" he shouted into the mike on the URC-4.

The sound of the F-51s faded as they flew on north.

"Son of a bitch!" he groaned.

"Jesus, they flew right on by us," rasped Wright, who had struggled to his feet beside DuPont. "Is the radio working?"

"I don't know."

"Grenadier Love! This is Pedro! This is Pedro! Do you read?" DuPont repeated his frantic call several times, with no answer.

"Hey, I hear them coming back!" said Fryer, who had also stumbled to his feet.

"Pedro, this is Grenadier Love. Do you read me?" said a clear voice on the radio.

Charlie DuPont let out a shout: "Yahoo! You bet I do!"

"I say, ole chap, it's good to hear you."

"Times that by ten, and you'll know how good it is to hear you, Grenadier Love!" barked Charlie.

"Good show. Are you okay?"

"Other than frozen stiff, we're fine. Are the choppers coming?"

"Righto. They are en route. Where are you?"

"We're just south of your position. You're coming toward us now. We're in the trees on the ridge just to your right."

"Roger. Tell me when I'm directly over you."

DuPont could see the F-51s approaching. "Turn left a little . . . okay, that's good . . . keep coming . . . a little more left . . . hold . . . you're almost there . . . now! You just passed directly over us!"

"Okay Pedro, I got you spotted. There are two choppers coming, and they should be here within the next thirty minutes. We'll set up a CAP over you until they get here."

"Grenadier Love, I suggest you keep an eye on our location but orbit a bit north of us. That should mislead any of our North Korean neighbors who might be interested in what's going on over here."

"Good idea, Pedro, we'll move north a little."

"And Grenadier Love, we should destroy the chopper. I hate to do it, but I don't want the commies to get hold of it."

"Righto, we'll take care of it."

"Oh man, I think we're gonna make it," said Fryer, leaning against a tree.

"Sure, we're gonna make it. I never had any doubt," said Charlie with a grin.

"Me either. I knew you Pedro guys would come through," added Wright, also smiling.

"I hope they got a hoist on those choppers, 'cause there ain't no way they can get us without one," said Fryer, glancing up at the trees.

Wouldn't that be a bummer, thought Charlie. "Grenadier Love, this is Pedro, would you check with JOC and make sure those choppers have a personnel hoist?"

"Pedro, this is Col. John Dean in Pedro Zero Two. Are you reading me?"

Charlie was surprised to hear the voice of his commander on the URC-4. "Roger, colonel, I read you."

Taken at K-16, Seoul, Korea, shortly after their escape from North Korea on October 26, 1951: (left to right) chopper pilot Lt. Charles DuPont, medic Gerald Fryer, downed F-80 pilot Vernon Wright, and chopper pilot Capt. Bob Barnhill. (Courtesy Charles J. DuPont)

"We've got a hoist, Charlie, and we'll be there in a few minutes to pick you up."

"That's great, colonel. We're gonna have to be hoisted out. When I hear you coming, I'll talk you into our location."

"Okay. Bob Barnhill is flying Pedro Zero One. He'll come in and get the first two. Then I'll come in and get you, ole buddy."

DuPont grinned. His commander had never referred to him as his "ole buddy" before, but under these circumstances that was just fine.

A few minutes later, the two Sikorsky H-5 helicopters came into view, and DuPont directed them to his location. While the South African CAP watched over them, the first chopper came in and lowered the "horse collar" [a circular, collar device that went under the arms to lift the survivor] on the cable. Joe Fryer and Vernon Wright were winched up, one at a time, to the helicopter, which hovered above the trees. Then the colonel in Pedro Zero Two picked up DuPont.

With Grenadier Love watching over them, the two choppers then flew out of North Korea and landed safely at K-16 in Seoul.

Korean War records indicate that this mission, flown on October 25 and 26, 1951, was the first successful rescue of a downed chopper crew in the Korean War. It was also one of thousands of rescue missions flown by U.S. Air Force helicopter crews in which pilots and aircrew, shot down in North Korea, were snatched from under the enemy's guns or from the waters of the Yellow Sea. The USAF Air Rescue Service was given credit for saving nearly 10,000 United Nations lives during the Korean War.

Lt. Charles DuPont was sent home after this mission, his ninety-first, and was recommended for the Distinguished Service Cross. I knew about Charlie's mission but needed some details to write the story. He gave me those details and a couple of additional anecdotes: He said the Grenadier Love leader told him afterward that they fired rockets and thousands of rounds of .50-caliber machine-gun fire into the fallen Sikorsky helicopter before they finally got it to burn. Charlie also admitted it took two days for him to thaw out, but that didn't bother him because that's how long he stayed inebriated.

3

Bluebird

Washington, D.C. 0903 hours. March 15, 1952.

When the buzzer sounded, John Mallory was so engrossed in the document he was reading, he reached across his desk without looking, picked up the phone, and put it to his ear. Before he could speak, the buzzer sounded again, this time piercing his concentration.

"Yeah?"

The buzzer rang again.

Mallory's eyes shot to the red phone on the table next to his desk. He dropped the white phone quickly and snatched up the red receiver.

"Mallory."

"Code red one!" snapped a voice.

"Red one?"

"Roger!"

"You're sure?"

"Confirmed! All stations alerted."

Mallory stabbed a switch on the red phone. After several rings a voice came on. "The chief is having a cup of coffee, John. This is the usual drill, right?"

"No! It's for real, go get him!"

"Are you serious?"

"Damn it, Mike. Yes, I'm serious! Get him and get him quick!"

"Okay, okay."

As Mallory waited for the White House chief of staff to come on the line, his thoughts spun. Could it actually be the real thing? It was hard to imagine that it was happening. Despite all the planning and testing, which they certainly had done in all seriousness, he hadn't really thought that a code red one—the signal that a nuclear attack on the United States was imminent—would ever actually come to pass. There had been lots of code red threes for practice, and even a couple of twos. But never a one.

"What is it, John?"

"Code red one!"

Hesitation. "A drill?"

"There is no drill on code red one, Bill."

"It's confirmed?"

"Yes. ADC [Air Defense Command] and SAC [Strategic Air Command] have been alerted. Notify the president!"

"He's on the *Sequoia*."

"Where are they?"

"They're down the river near Colonial Beach."

"Damn! Wouldn't you know this would happen when he's out of pocket."

"Do you think it's the real thing, John?"

"God, I don't know, Bill. Command says it is."

"Then we need the president back here quick."

"Yeah, you're right. I'll activate Bluebird."

Langley Air Force Base, Virginia. 0904 hours.

I was the alert duty pilot, sitting in a little cubbyhole in base operations, talking to one of the other pilots in our select group, Capt. Pierce Myers. Pierce was telling me a story about the elderly black maitre d' at the Langley Officers Club who had been there since the early days of the Army Air Corps. It seemed that Air Force Gen. Hap Arnold came into the club one day during World War Two and the maitre d' said, "Well, hello there Lieutenant Arnold, I haven't seen you around here for quite a spell."

"That's a great story," I said, laughing.

"Yeah. He knew all those early Air Corps pilots, including Billy Mitchell. One of the guys was telling me that he—"

The buzzer on my red phone shrieked.

Pierce and I looked at each other. I snatched it up and said, "Bluebird."

"Scramble Bluebird, code red one," instructed a voice.

"Red one?" It was an instinctive reaction, since I'd just assumed that I would never hear those words.

"Repeat: code red one!" snapped the voice on the line.

"Yes, sir!" I said and quickly punched the alert button, grabbed my "Mae West" [life vest] and headed for the front door of base operations.

The alert crew, responding to my signal, was already hurriedly removing the rotor blade tie-down ropes as I ran up to the Sikorsky H-5 helicopter parked out on the flight ramp. I quickly climbed into the cockpit, fastened my safety belt, and flipped on the master switch.

The alert crew chief, standing beside the helicopter with a fire bottle, gave me a thumbs-up and a smile. I'm sure he assumed it was the usual practice drill. When he saw the look on my face, however, his smile dissolved.

As required, the helicopter was already preflighted, full of fuel, and ready to go. I hit the starter and the Pratt & Whitney R-985 coughed, spit out a column of black smoke, and roared to life. As instruments stabilized and temperatures climbed, I punched the radio button and slipped on my headset.

"Langley tower, this is Bluebird," I transmitted excitedly. On routine flights we called the tower with our aircraft number. On an operational scramble, we were instructed to use Bluebird, which told the tower operator that we rated a priority over other traffic. This was my first such application.

There was no answer from the tower for a moment. I sensed the hesitation: "Was that Bluebird calling Langley tower?"

"Roger, Bluebird," I confirmed.

No hesitation now. "Roger, Bluebird, clear for immediate takeoff. All traffic at Langley Air Force Base, be advised we have a priority aircraft departing northbound."

"Roger, tower," I replied, then revved the Sikorsky up to takeoff RPM and pulled pitch.

There was a burgeoning excitement stirring inside me as I headed north on a special departure route. As soon as I'd cleared the air base I punched the button on my VHF radio that put me on a discreet frequency.

"Eagle control, this is Bluebird," I transmitted.

"Roger, Bluebird, activate squawk now," came the quick reply.

"Roger, wilco," I replied, flipping the switch on another black box that had been installed next to my VHF radio.

After a few moments: "We got you, Bluebird. Take a heading of 340 degrees and climb to angels three" [an altitude of three thousand feet].

I repeated the instructions, took up the heading, and put the H-5 into a climb. I saw the York River below me now, and my peripheral vision picked up the Yorktown monument commemorating Washington's victory over Cornwallis, which had saved the republic. And then came a jolting thought: I had been scrambled on a code red one! Did that mean what I assumed it meant? An attack on the United States was imminent. I glanced down at the monument again, and suddenly I envisioned what I had seen on Eniwetok.

I'd been a helicopter pilot on Eniwetok Atoll during "Operation Greenhouse" in 1951 and saw a nuclear bomb turn an entire city into a smoldering wasteland. As those images flashed through my memory now, a cold fear gripped me, and the terrible reality of the mission I was flying struck me like a sledgehammer.

When the atomic-bomb tests on Eniwetok Atoll were completed in June 1951, I was reassigned to the 4415th Air Base Group at Pope Air Force Base, North Carolina. It was good to be home with my wife and two sons again after a year's separation. I was assigned as a helicopter instructor and was lucky enough to get on-base housing at nearby Fort Bragg. It was good duty, and I was enjoying the assignment, until one day a few months later when my commander called me in and said that I was being sent TDY [temporary duty] to Langley Air Force Base in Virginia.

I was not a happy camper because TDY meant another separation from my family. There were no provisions for dependent travel when the sponsor was sent on temporary duty. To make it worse, my commander said he didn't have a clue as to why I was being sent or how long I would be gone.

When I got to Langley, I reported to a major who had come down from the Pentagon to brief me. I can't remember his name, but the briefing went something like this:

"Captain Kirkland, you have been selected for this project because of your qualifications. You are an experienced helicopter pilot, correct?"

"Yes, sir."

"You have a top-secret clearance?"

"Yes, sir."

"And you participated in nuclear-weapons testing on Operation Greenhouse?"

"Yes, sir."

"Not a word of this briefing is to go out of this room. Do you understand?"

"Yes, sir."

The major nodded, dug a pack of cigarettes out of his blouse pocket, and offered me one. I accepted and we both lit up and blew clouds of smoke in the small office in one corner of Langley Base Operations. That was before we knew that cigarette smoke was almost as bad as radioactive fallout.

"This office is the duty station for the special unit to which you have been assigned. You and three other helicopter pilots will rotate on twenty-four-hour alert duty. You must be ready to pilot a helicopter as instructed by a controller on a discreet radio frequency. Your initial alert will come through this telephone," said the major, touching a red telephone on the desk.

I glanced at the phone. Since the Cold War started I'd heard stories about red telephones associated with the SAC alert crews. But they were flying the giant B-36s with atomic bombs aboard to retaliate in the event of a nuclear attack. Why would the Air Force want helicopters on a red-phone alert?

The major took a puff of his cigarette and looked at me. "This is a very important mission, captain. And I want you to recognize that."

"Yes, sir. What is it?"

"All information is top secret and on a need-to-know basis."

"I need to know what I'm supposed to do, sir."

"I'm coming to that."

"Yes, sir."

"Your function is to transport VIP in an emergency. When alerted, you will proceed as directed by an air controller to a specific destination, pick up a passenger or possibly two, and fly them to another destination as specified by the controller."

"Another taxi service, huh?"

The major frowned at me.

"Uh, that is what I was doing on Eniwetok: a helicopter taxi service for VIP."

"Captain, I can assure you this is more than a taxi service. The VIP you will be carrying is *the* VIP."

"What?"

"Never mind. Forget I said that. All you need to know is that you are to follow the instructions of the controller, understood?"

"Yes, sir. But what if I lose radio contact?"

"The helicopter has been equipped with redundant radio systems. Total failure is not likely. Any further questions?"

"Well, I'd like to know a little more of what I—"

"You have all the information you need, captain."

"Yes, sir, but—"

1st Lt. Richard Kirkland at Langley Air Force Base, Virginia, standing beside "Bluebird" Sikorsky H-5, March 1952.

"If you are incapacitated for any reason, you are to call me at this number on the regular telephone." The major scribbled a number on a notepad and handed it to me. "You are not to touch the red phone unless it rings."

We both looked at the red phone.

"You will receive periodic calls and be dispatched on missions classified as code two or three. You will not receive a code one unless it's the real thing, and it will be identified to you as 'code red one.'"

"The real thing?"

"An operational mission requiring you to transport a VIP."

I looked at the major questioningly.

". . . of the highest priority," he added.

I nodded.

The major glanced at his watch, ground out his cigarette, and got up from the chair. "Let's hope you never get a code red one, captain," he said, and walked out of the room.

Command Center, Pentagon. 0915 hours. March 15, 1952.

Maj. Gen. Robert Moody, U.S. Air Force, stood watching the technicians hovering around a huge transparent map in the cavernous command control room, their headset chords trailing behind as they made notations with a grease pencil.

"Bob, where are we?" came the urgent voice of a four-star Air Force general who hurried into the glass-enclosed cubicle.

Moody turned and faced the four star. "All stations of Air Force, Navy, and Army deterrent systems are on red alert, as are all ADC and SAC aircraft."

"The president?"

"The White House has been notified. But we don't have confirmation."

"What?"

"They haven't confirmed contact with the president."

"What's holding them up?"

"I don't know."

"Did you contact Mallory?"

"Yes, sir. He says they're working on it."

"Jesus Christ! They're working on it? Don't they realize how serious this is?"

"I think they do, but the president is on the *Sequoia,* and I got a feeling they have some kind of communications problem."

The four star shook his head. "I was afraid of this. I told that fathead Mallory they should—"

A screeching buzzer interrupted the two generals, and Moody grabbed the red phone. "Moody," he barked. After listening a moment, he nodded and replaced the red receiver. "Bluebird has been activated."

"Bluebird?"

"You know, the helicopter."

"The helicopter?"

"Yes. It's supposed to pick up the president in an emergency and take him to the command center."

Presidential yacht *Sequoia*. Potomac River. 0919 hours.

Assistant to the president Col. William Scott hurried down the polished passageway, nodded to the Secret Service agent on duty, and stepped out onto the aft deck of the *Sequoia*.

"Mr. President."

President Harry Truman looked up from where he sat in a deck chair reading. "Yes, what is it, Scotty?"

"Sorry to disturb you, sir, but we have a problem that I think you should be aware of."

"Well, you know my motto: 'The buck stops here,'" said the president, smiling.

Scott forced a little smile and nodded. "Yes, sir. The problem is that our entire communications system on *Sequoia* is inoperative, and we've lost contact with the command center."

"That doesn't surprise me. The trouble nowadays is that all this high-tech stuff is too complicated and when it goes ker-put you're up shit creek without a paddle."

"Yes, sir. The problem here is—"

"When I was in France in World War One, we got our info direct. None of this electronic stuff that's always shootin craps for some damn reason or another."

"Yes, sir. I'm sure it's a temporary thing, and they'll have it fixed shortly, but meanwhile . . . if there should be an alert. . . ?"

Truman nodded. "Yep, you're right. I guess we better head for the barn."

"Yes, sir. I'll so advise the captain."

Near Tappahannock, Virginia. 0939 hours.

When I spotted the Potomac River over the nose of the helicopter, it was a lead-gray color reflected by the dull overcast that had gradually lowered on the horizon. Since the H-5 helicopter was not equipped for instrument flight, I'd been forced to lower my flight altitude to less than one thousand feet.

"Bluebird, this is Eagle Control. Are you receiving me?"

"Roger, Eagle, I read you," I replied.

"Bluebird, you're so low you're erratic on the scope, can't you get some more altitude?"

"Can't do it, Eagle. I'm already flying in scud along the bottom of the overcast."

Silence.

"Bluebird, turn left to a new heading of 270 degrees. That might get you into an area of a little higher ceiling."

"Roger, 270 degrees."

I banked the helicopter around, but within a few minutes I could tell the overcast was even lower to the west.

"Eagle, this is Bluebird. The weather is worse on this heading."

"Roger, Bluebird. Stand by."

Silence.

"Bluebird, turn right to a new heading of 090 degrees."

"Roger, Eagle, 090 degrees."

A few minutes later I spotted the Potomac River again in the distance, and, although there was a light mist hanging from the overcast, I was able to maintain enough altitude to stay out of the clouds.

"Bluebird, this is Eagle, we've lost you on the scope. Where are you?"

"Eagle, I'm coming up on the Potomac River."

"Bluebird, can you follow the river northwest?"

"I'm gonna give it try, Eagle."

"Bluebird, be reminded this is a code red one, operational mission."

"I know, Eagle. I know."

I knew all right, and it had weighed heavy on my mind since hearing the words over the red phone. Could it actually be true? Was a nuclear attack really coming? I had never actually been told that a code red one meant that. But it was a logical assumption, since the major had left little doubt who my VIP passenger would be if it happened. And there was a lot of talk those days about the nuclear threat, because the war in Korea was going on with communist Russia and China supporting North Korea. But then, maybe I was over reacting. I hoped so.

Command Center, Pentagon. 0941 hours.

Gen. Robert Moody snatched the red phone as it screeched. "Yeah."

"General, we're at a point of no return. We've got to have a decision."

"Tell me about it. I don't have a decision. There is a communications breakdown, and we can't contact the president. It has paralyzed the whole damn system!"

"What are we gonna do?"

"There's nothing to do until we reestablish communications and get in contact with the president. He's the only one who can make the decision."

"Well, what are they doing about it?"

"They're working on it."

"Yeah."

"Meanwhile, Bluebird is en route."

"We really gonna do that?"

"That was the Bluebird plan, wasn't it?"

"Yes, sir. But as you know, that was just window dressing. Nobody really figured we'd ever actually do it."

"Well, it looks like our window dressing is gonna play center stage in this fiasco."

Near Colonial Beach, Virginia. 0945 hours.

The sky had turned a threatening shade of gray, the ceiling had lowered even more, and the mist streaked across my windshield. It seemed to mirror my feelings of pending doom. But I still had a three-hundred-foot ceiling and about a half mile visibility, which is enough for helicopter flying.

"Bluebird, this is Eagle, where are you?" cracked the controller's voice in my headset.

"I'm approaching Colonial Beach, Eagle."

"Stand by, Bluebird."

"Roger."

Thirty seconds later: "Bluebird from Eagle. Continue up the river. There is an installation at Dahlgren with a boat dock on the river. It will be your initial destination. Report when you have it in sight."

"Roger, Eagle."

Sequoia. Potomac River. 0946 hours.

Seaman First Class Daniel Martin hurried down the passageway and onto the *Sequoia* lounge where Colonel Scott and a couple of the president's guests were visiting and drinking coffee.

"Colonel Scott, sir, this message just came over our ship-to-shore radio. It's addressed to you, sir."

"Thank you," said the colonel. One glance told Scott it was coded. He excused himself, went to his cabin, and quickly decoded the message. Then he hurried down the passageway to the president's cabin, knocked, and was invited in.

"Sir, we just received a coded message on ship-to-shore radio recommending that, because of our communications breakdown with the command center, we dock at the Army installation at Dahlgren."

The president, sitting at a desk, hesitated. "We're still out of contact with the command center?"

"Yes, sir. I'm afraid so."

President Truman nodded. "Yep, the way things are right now with those sons of bitches over there, we better not take any chances."

"Yes, sir. I'll advise the captain. Oh, and the message also said that Bluebird has been activated."

"Bluebird?"

"Yes, sir. That's the helicopter to provide emergency transportation for you."

"Oh, sure. I remember now. Well, I think it's a good idea to go ahead and dock, just to be on the safe side, but I don't know that I need a helicopter."

"It was probably dispatched as a precautionary thing."

"Yeah, probably. You ever fly in one, Scotty?"

"No, sir."

The president leaned back in his chair. "You know, it would be kinda fun to take a spin around town in one of those things. And wouldn't Bess have a shit fit if I came flying in and landed on the front lawn of the White House in that contraption?" said the president, breaking into a grin.

Over Dahlgren, Virginia. 0947 hours.

Flying at about three hundred feet, I was following the shoreline of the Potomac River with both the weather and my anxiety getting worse by the minute, when I spotted the Dahlgren dock. As I approached, I eased off on the collective and started a gentle circle to scan the area for wires and obstacles.

It wouldn't be long now, and I would know who my VIP passenger was. Would it really be the president? Probably. That stirred the excitement—and the reality: if it was him, it would also mean that something bad was going on, like a nuclear attack.

"Bluebird, this is Eagle. Do you have your destination in sight?" cracked the voice in my headset.

"Roger, Eagle. I got it."

"Is it suitable for landing, Bluebird?"

"It is suitable."

"Good work, Bluebird. Stand by for instructions."

"Roger."

Sequoia. Potomac River. 0948 hours.

Michael Kelly, Secret Service agent in charge of the presidential security on the *Sequoia,* shook his head grimly. "I can't believe they're even considering this madness."

"You mean the helicopter, uh, Bluebird?" said agent Jeff Miller, the other Secret Service agent aboard the ship.

"That's exactly what I mean."

"Well, I'm sure it won't actually come to pass. It's just a precautionary exercise," said Miller, standing beside Kelly in the yacht's small control center.

"I know, but it makes me nervous. That program is only supposed to be activated in case of a code red one."

"Yes, but with command communications down, I guess they figure an alert could happen and the president would be out of touch. I think that's what they are concerned about."

"That's true. But from a security standpoint, putting the president of the United States in a single-engine aircraft to putsy out across the countryside is pure madness."

Miller nodded. "Yeah, I have to agree with that."

"After all there's no code red one in effect."

"Well, there could be."

Hesitation. "Yeah. That's true. In fact, when I stop to think about it, the chief wasn't all that thrilled about using a helicopter, so he sure wouldn't authorize Bluebird unless . . . Jesus! You don't suppose?"

Command Center, Pentagon. 0950 hours.

Lt. Col. Ray Benning pushed open the glass door of the general's cubicle without knocking and shouted breathlessly: "General Moody! Code red one is canceled!"

Moody looked at the officer incredulously. "What did you say?"

"It's canceled, sir. The signal just came in from ADC HQ Command."

"How . . . what?" The general grabbed the red phone on his console and punched the button. "ADC Commander," he growled.

After a moment. "What the hell is going on, Kevin?"

Another moment of listening. "Christ, Kevin, how could that be?"

More listening. "All right, all right. Get things shut down, and I'll talk to you later." The general set the red phone back in its cradle and looked at Benning. "Old Murphy's Law has really been in full swing today," he said, shaking his head, then added: "But thank God it was Murphy instead of the real thing." [Murphy's Law: If something can go wrong, it will.]

Approaching Dahlgren, Virginia. 0953 hours.

Col. William Scott stepped up to the polished wooden door of the presidential suite and knocked. "Come in," said the president.

Scott opened the door and stepped inside. "Mr. President, we'll be docking in a few minutes."

"Okay. I'm ready. Have the secretary and the others been advised?"

"Yes, sir. They are on deck and ready to debark."

"Okay, I'll go up and join them," said President Truman, getting up from the desk where he had been writing.

"You may want to slip on a jacket, Mr. President. It turned a bit nippy on deck."

A few minutes later, President Truman and Colonel Scott left the suite. "Doggone, the weather did turn a little sour on us didn't it?" said the president as they walked out under the canvas awning on the yacht's aft deck.

"Yes, sir, it sure did," said Scott.

"Sorry our cruise got interrupted, fellows," said President Truman, as he joined the secretary of state and a small group of his other guests. "We got a little problem with both the weather and our communications, so to make sure all the bases are covered we had to make a change in the schedule."

At the sudden sound of beating rotor blades overhead, everyone glanced up.

"By Jove, there he is, sure enough," said the president.

"What is it?" asked the secretary of state.

"Why that's Bluebird, my taxi service back to Washington," said President Truman, grinning broadly.

Secret Service agent Michael Kelly gasped and turned pale.

Over Dahlgren, Virginia. 0959 hours.

As I circled the Potomac River dock at Dahlgren, I was scanning my landing area so intently that I evidently flew right over the top of the *Sequoia* without seeing it. On the dock, there were armed weapons carriers, jeeps, and soldiers in full battle dress. It was the type of scene you would expect with a code red one in effect. And I knew with a sudden, terrible certainty who my passenger was.

"Bluebird, this is Eagle."

"Roger, Eagle. I'm preparing to land."

"Bluebird, this is Eagle. Code red one is canceled. Do not land. Your mission is terminated. Return to station."

"What?"

"I repeat, Bluebird. Do not land. Your mission is canceled. Take up a heading of 163 degrees."

I sat there in the cockpit of the Sikorsky helicopter for a couple of minutes. What in the world had happened? Was this all some kind of a joke? One minute a nuclear attack on the United States is imminent and I'm about to fly the president. The next moment a stoic voice says it's all canceled, go home.

"Bluebird, this is Eagle, acknowledge your new heading please."

"Uh, repeat, Eagle?"

"Your heading, Bluebird, is 163 degrees."

Silence.

"Eagle, this is Bluebird. What's going on here?" I transmitted. I shouldn't have, but I did.

Silence.

"Look at it this way, Bluebird: it's better than the alternative."

I thought about it for a moment and realized that, obviously, code red one had started out as the real thing, then someone, somewhere in all that complex structure of thousands of men and women involved in the defense of our country, discovered that it wasn't the real thing.

"Yeah, you're right, Eagle," I said.

Memory wouldn't provide me with some of the details involving call signs, timing, and such, so I improvised. But my role in the story is the way I remember it. The action at the command center, the White House, and on the Sequoia is how I envisioned it might have happened. As it turned out, a real code red one never came, fortunately, and President Truman never did get his spin around town in the helicopter. President Eisenhower was the first to fly in a helicopter on July 13, 1957. It was an Air Force Bell VH-13J. President Kennedy was the first president to use the helicopter regularly. Since then, it has been a common sight in Washington to see Marine One, *a big twin-jet Sikorsky, coming and going from the White House lawn.*

4

Battlefield Taxi

Inside a "mummy" sleeping bag with all my clothes on except my boots, I was still cold. I'd heard someone the day before say that it was the coldest winter in Korea since 1840. I wasn't there in 1840, but I doubt it could have been any colder than it was that December 1952.

It was early morning, and four of us Air Force helicopter pilots were huddled in our sleeping bags in a GI pyramidal tent at the 8055 MASH [Mobile Army Surgical Hospital]. We were close enough to the 38th parallel, where the battle line ran, that we could hear artillery rumbling off in the distance. How those guys could get out of bed in that bitter cold and start shooting at each other was beyond my imagination.

Our field phone was in a canvas case hanging on a two-by-four that ran down the side of the tent. It didn't really ring, it sort of diddled. But it shattered the early morning tranquility of our canvas igloo, sounding like a four-alarm fire to me, because it meant I had to crawl out of my sack and try to coax a frozen helicopter into flying to a frozen Korean battlefield to pick up some poor GI who now had bullet holes in him.

"You're next up, Kirkland," mumbled our element commander from inside his sleeping bag.

"Yeah, I'm going," I mumbled back, unzipping the sleeping bag and grabbing my boots.

"Turn up the fuel on the stove," grumbled one of the other pilots.

"It's already as high as it'll go," I replied, pulled on my heavy winter parka, and jerked the field phone from its case. "8055 chopper."

Capt. Richard Kirkland and medic, with wounded GI in litter pod attached to Sikorsky H-5. We had just picked up the patient from the Korean battlefield and landed at 8055 MASH, winter 1952–53.

"Pickup a casualty at 23 Baker, 8055."

I pulled the gridded map out of my jacket pocket and quickly checked the designated pick-up point. "Check, 23 Baker. Any change in the MLR?" I asked.

"No change in the past twenty-four hours."

It was critical for me to know if the MLR [main line of resistance] had changed during the night, since the only way I could get my battlefield taxi to the pick-up point without getting shot down was to fly through the bottom of a canyon that was in friendly territory. Although the MLR never varied more than a few miles during the last two years of the Korean War, it did change often enough for historians to refer to that period of the war as the Battle of the Hills, because of the shifting ownership of such places as Old Baldy, Porkchop Hill, and Heartbreak Ridge.

Intelligence was supposed to keep us posted of changes, but that didn't always happen, and we would find ourselves flying over the guys in green uniforms who shot holes in our helicopter with lead balls made in North Korea, and the choppers of that day were totally unarmed and had no armor protection whatever.

"Okay, I'm on my way," I said, dropped the phone back in the canvas case, and headed out the door.

As I stepped out of the tent, I recognized the bundled-up figure coming across the compound. It was Hawkeye. "What are you doing up this early, Hawk?" I asked.

He pushed his parka hood up and peeked out at me. "Oh, I just love strolling in the early morning on such a beautiful day in breathtaking Korea," he chirped, his breath coming out in puffs of little white clouds.

I laughed, even though I wasn't in the mood. But that was the way Hawkeye was. No matter how bad things got, he never seemed to lose his sense of humor. I have always believed that his humor played a major role in the morale of the 8055 MASH. Often, when those fine doctors, nurses, and corpsmen worked around the clock saving the lives of wounded GIs, Hawkeye's humor kept them going. Even when he himself was about to drop from exhaustion, he still cracked jokes. Hawk's real name, incidently, was Sam Gilfand. He was an outstanding surgeon from New York City, and a great guy. The folks who wrote the television series *M**A**S***H* did a pretty good job. Some of the characters were a bit Hollywoody, but a lot of it was pretty close to the way it was at the 8055 MASH.

"I suppose you're on your way to bring us some business this fine morning, huh, ace?" He always called me "ace," even though I wasn't. But he knew I'd been a fighter pilot and shot down a couple Zeros in World War Two. He claimed I looked like an ace anyway.

"That's what I'm fixing to do, Hawk," I said over my shoulder as I hurried toward the helipad.

"Yes. Heavens to Betsy and four hands around, we wouldn't want this fine establishment to be without customers," he sort of said to no one in particular as he pulled his parka hood back down and walked off toward the OR, where he was probably on the early shift.

The crew chief on duty had managed to pry open the frozen helicopter door by the time I got out to the helipad, but that 1940s model Sikorsky H-5 was so cold it actually creaked and groaned when I climbed up into the pilot's seat. It was a good bird for its vintage. But it wasn't designed to operate in subzero weather.

"The battery won't last long this morning, captain," advised the chief as he rolled a portable fire extinguisher beside the helicopter.

I nodded. I knew I'd only get one shot at starting the engine, but I must have had the magic touch that morning because after a couple of coughs, she spit out a column of black smoke and roared to life. The chief gave me a thumbs-up and backed off the helipad as my medic came running up, his medical kit slung over his shoulder. He had on so much bulky clothing he couldn't climb into the back-seat, so the chief had to help him in.

It seemed to take forever before temperature and pressure gauges all showed green. Finally, I pulled pitch and nosed the H-5 north toward medical pick-up spot 23 Baker on the Korean battlefield.

In World War Two the Army Medical Corps practiced a battlefield system called Triage, which was based on the brutally realistic fact that front-line surgeons could treat three or four walking wounded in the same amount of time required for one seriously wounded, so they were treated last. Then they had to endure a long, jarring ambulance ride to the field hospital. As a consequence, the mortality rate for the seriously wounded was high.

That all changed in the Korean War when the MASH was introduced. It consisted of a team of surgeons, anesthesiologists, nurses, and corpsmen, and the necessary equipment, that gave them the mobility to deploy and function on the fringe of the battlefield. The wounded were taxied by helicopter from the front-line aid stations directly to the hospital within minutes. Not only did the mortality rates drop dramatically, but military historians credit the helicopter-supported MASH with the greatest single boost to battlefield morale in modern warfare.

Although there were only a handful available, Korea was opening night for helicopters on the battlefield, and both the U.S. Air Force and Army deployed them for front-line MASH medevac [medical evacuation]. Army pilots flew the Bell H-13, and Air Force pilots flew the Sikorsky H-5 and H-19.

I was assigned to the 2157th Air Force, Air Rescue Squadron, at Kimpo Air Base (K-16) at Seoul. The squadron kept four helicopter pilots, four medics, a couple of mechanics, and at least one H-5 at the 8055 MASH full time. We lived with them in their tent city, and when they moved, we moved, helicopter and all.

The H-5 had three fabric-covered rotor blades powered by a Pratt & Whitney 450-horsepower engine. The "chopper," as it was called in Korea, had two seats: a pilot's seat up front and a passenger's seat directly behind where the medic rode. The medic's job was to perform whatever emergency medical aid that was necessary to stabilize a patient, then load him into the personnel pod

Dr. Sam Gilfand (facing camera), alias "Hawkeye," at the 8055 MASH, Korea, winter 1953.

[an aluminum carrying case] attached to the side of the helicopter. Barring interference from the bad guys, we then flew him from the battlefield to the MASH, where he would be under the care of well-equipped surgeons within minutes.

After takeoff, that brutally cold morning, I kept my eye on the instruments for awhile even though the bird seemed to be functioning normally. The controls, although a bit stiff, were responding. So I set the friction on the throttle and the collective, to hold power, and pulled out my map. Identifying the correct canyon at the outset was the key to finding the pick-up spot without running into the North Koreans.

In the subzero cockpit, it was difficult to even hold a map with gloved hands, and studying it with all the cumulus clouds my breath was creating added to the problem. I had the heater on full blast, but it wasn't doing much. On the plus side, it was a crystal-clear day, and I knew, at this point anyway, that I was in the right canyon to intersect the 38th parallel.

I had to fly below the top of the ridges to stay out of enemy gunsight while keeping a sharp watch for the branch canyon that would take me east to the aid station at 23 Baker. Although I had made several pickups at that spot, it wasn't easy to find. After two years of artillery fire, bombs, and mortars the ridges and canyons were so battle scarred they all looked alike.

"I think this is where we want to go," I said to my medic on the intercom, as I banked into a small canyon. He mumbled something in reply. Glancing back at him, all I could see was a bundle of clothing hunched down in the backseat.

I was reasonably confident I had turned into the right canyon until my medic suddenly came alive and began to screech over the intercom: "They're shooting at us captain! They're shooting at us!"

I quickly looked out my side canopy window, and, sure enough, he was right: guys in green uniforms were shooting at us. I could even see the little white clouds their rifles made when they fired into the frigid air. So much for the twenty-four-hour intelligence report, I thought, as I slammed the chopper into a quick right bank and zipped over the ridge into the adjacent canyon. Later, intelligence told me that it was a North Korean patrol that had gotten themselves lost—they were the ones in the wrong canyon, not me.

After a short detour and some anxious moments, I got back into the right canyon again and landed a few minutes later at 23 Baker. Usually, I wouldn't shut the bird down at the pickup point. I would stay in the pilot's seat with the rotors turning and smoke a quick cigarette while the medics loaded the patient, then we'd be off. In this case I was concerned that some of those North Korean lead balls may have disturbed the integrity of my taxicab, so I kept the engine running but disengaged the rotor so I could get out and take a look.

The good news was that I couldn't find any damage to the bird. The bad new was that they had three seriously wounded patients at the aid station, and the H-5 could only carry two patients and a medic.

"All three are critical, and, with the temperature where it is, they won't last long," said a grim Army corpsmen dressed in winter clothes and combat gear. Automatic weapons opened fire about that time in the near distance. I winced, but the corpsmen seemed to not even notice.

"I'm sorry," I said, "I'll have to make another trip. I can't carry—"

"Are they conscious?" interrupted my medic.

The corpsmen shook his head. "They're pretty much out of it."

"Okay. We can put one in the litter and give the other two stiff shots of morphine and strap them into the backseat," said my medic, glancing at me through the slit in his parka hood.

"And, what are you gonna do?" I asked.

"I'll stay here, and you can come back and get me."

I glanced at the Army medic.

He shrugged. The weariness in his parka-shrouded face was evident. "The gooks are on a roll, and they could overrun us," he said calmly.

I can't remember the name of my medic that day, but he was a brave young man. He said, "If it's okay with you, captain, I'll stay."

I hesitated.

"It's worth the gamble to save a man's life," he added. And I knew he was sincere.

"Okay, let's get them loaded," I said, with a good deal of apprehension.

They gave the badly wounded patients heavy doses of morphine, wrapped them in as many blankets as they could, put one in the external pod, and strapped the other two into the backseat of the helicopter.

"They'll be out for quite awhile, capt'n, so you shouldn't have any trouble," said the Army corpsmen.

"Okay. I'll be back as soon as I can make it," I said to my medic.

"I'll be right here," he said with a grin.

"We'll try to keep him entertained," said the corpsmen, and he managed a grin too.

I nodded, closed the door, and flipped the clutch-engagement lever. As soon as the rotor was up and turning at takeoff RPM, I pulled pitch and scooted down the canyon as fast as the bird would go.

There was just something about going off and leaving my medic that really upset me. I understood his reasoning. It was a brave thing for him to do, and his action could well save a man's life. But it could also cost the medic his life if 23 Baker was overrun by the North Koreans. So I wanted to deliver the patients to the MASH as fast as possible and get back to pick him up.

Everything went well for the first few minutes of the flight. I glanced back into the rear seat, and the patients were strapped in tight, and still unconscious. Then, just as I banked into the main canyon that would take me to the MASH, I heard a God-awful cry and something akin to a sledgehammer struck the back of my head. The force of the blow jammed my arm forward, which caused the cyclic stick to shoot forward, launching the helicopter into a nose dive. That somehow tore the fire extinguisher from its bracket, and, naturally, it also ricocheted off my head.

Now I was seeing stars, and the helicopter was diving toward the Korean landscape. I managed to pull out of the dive, but I did it so violently the bird shot straight up on its tail. There were all kinds of weird noises in my head, weird sights before my eyes, and even weirder sounds coming from the Sikorsky H-5. I managed to kick rudder pedal, causing the bird to swap ends, and now I was going straight down again.

I'm not sure how many oscillations I made, or how close I came to hitting the Korean earth, before I finally got the helicopter under control. But about that time I heard another one of those God-awful cries, and I instinctively ducked as another blow struck the back of the seat. I glanced back and saw that one of the patients had gained consciousness and was thrashing about, kicking wildly, and trying to pull himself loose from the seat straps.

I flipped open my safety belt and leaned as far forward as I could to keep away from his kicking feet, while trying to maintain some kind of control over the gyrating helicopter. The poor man's eyes were glazed and wild looking, and he was letting out one awful cry after another. He'd kicked off all the blankets and tore loose his bandages so that blood from his wounds was spewing in all directions as he thrashed around violently.

I knew I had to do something quick or we would all be in big trouble, because it was impossible to control the helicopter in the awkward position I had taken to avoid his vicious kicking. And I also realized that it was going to be impossible to land under these conditions without crashing. But I had no choice. I had to either pull out my .45 pistol and shoot the poor guy or try to land.

Since I couldn't shoot him, I lowered the collective and watched for the ground coming up from where I crouched between the seat and the instrument console. My head was still spinning, courtesy of the fire extinguisher, and my perspective was askew because of the position I was in. It would primarily be guesswork when to pull pitch. And that Korean landscape was frozen hard as a rock.

When I saw the ground coming up fast, I instinctively scrambled back into the pilot's seat, pulled pitch, and leveled the Sikorsky with cyclic. It was just something I did without thinking. My instincts would not allow the helicopter to crash. I cringed, anticipating the blow from the kicking feet. Then, after a second or two, I realized the kicking had stopped. I glanced back and saw that he was slumped over and unconscious.

I went down on the collective and back on the cyclic in one swift movement, executing a quick stop to a hover and then a landing. I chopped the throttle and just sat there a second or two, breathing a sigh of relief, thankful to be on the cold Korean earth in one piece and that was where I was going to stay. Then I looked out through the front canopy and saw a bunch of olive drab tents about a quarter mile down the canyon. One of them had a big red cross on the top—the 8055 MASH. I twisted on the throttle, eased up on the collective, and gently hover-taxied down the canyon to the helipad.

"Holly schmolly ace, I have the feeling you got a war story to tell," said Hawkeye as he and the corpsmen swung open the door and saw the patients in the blood-splattered backseat of the Sikorsky.

"You could say that, Hawk," I replied, swinging down from the pilot's seat and making a beeline for the male officer's quarters. When I opened the wooden door to my tent, the other three pilots were huddled around the stove in their winter clothes smoking cigarettes.

"Everything go okay?" asked my element commander, Capt. Charles Enderton.

"Not exactly," I said, grabbing the field phone and turning the crank. "I had to leave my medic and that sector is under attack."

"You went off and left the medic?" said Enderton incredulously.

"Yes, but . . . Get me G-2 quick!" I said to the field operator, then looked at Enderton. "It's a long story and . . ."

"It better damn well be a good one," he growled.

"G-2. Major Thompson," came the voice on the field phone.

"Sir, this is Captain Kirkland at the 8055 MASH. Can I get to 23 Baker?"

"23 Baker? Hold on."

I dug out a cigarette and fired it.

The loudspeaker outside in the compound started squealing as somebody tried to make an announcement.

Finally: "Uh, we're not sure. Our latest is that they are under fire, but we've had no recent reports."

"Then you don't know if they've been overrun?"

"No, we don't know. They call you for a pick-up?"

"Yeah. I was just up there."

"Were they under fire?"

"Yeah."

"Well then you know as much as we do."

"Yeah. . . . Okay, thanks anyway," I said and dropped the phone back in the canvas case.

"What's going on?" asked Enderton.

I took a big drag of the cigarette and ground it out in a 90mm shell casing we used as an ashtray. "I'm goin back to 23 Baker and pick up my medic," I said, zipped up my parka, and slammed out through the wooden front door.

When I got out to the heliport, the patients had been rushed into pre-op and the crew chief was there looking at the blood splattered backseat.

"Jesus, Capt'n, what happened?" he asked.

"I'll tell ya later, chief. I gotta go."

He nodded and looked at me strangely. "You know the fire extinguisher is lying in the backseat?"

I felt the knot on the back of my skull. "Yeah, I know, chief. Would you put it back in the bracket while I get the bird started?"

I took off a couple minutes later and headed up the canyon with a vague idea of what I intended to do when I reached 23 Baker. As I skimmed along the bottom of the canyon, I tried to solidify a couple of alternative plans of actions, but my still-aching head wasn't processing information well. Actually, I only had two options. If the North Koreans were there, they would shoot at me and I'd run. What else could I do? If they weren't there, I'd simply land and pick up my medic. It was that simple. But what if I couldn't tell, and, when I landed, they took me prisoner? I'd heard some spine-chilling stories of what a North Korean prison camp was like.

I detoured around the spot where I'd taken fire on the last trip and found 23 Baker without a problem. As I approached, I slowed down to a hover-taxi and gradually edged up toward the spot. I couldn't see any smoke from artillery fire, and everywhere I looked appeared peaceful and quiet. The outside air-temperature gauge still showed below zero. Maybe everybody decided it was too cold to fight, and they were all in their bunkers having tea and smoking cigarettes.

As it turned out, that's exactly what they were doing. The North Koreans had backed off their assault, and the GIs were, indeed, in their bunkers thawing out. And when I landed, they talked me into shutting down the bird and coming into one of their bunkers for some hot tea. I'm glad I did, because it was a unique experience. The bunker was surprisingly comfortable, and warmer than I would have imagined. It was partially underground and crude, but it had a kind of homey touch with a little gasoline stove and even pictures of loved ones on the sand-bagged walls. It was their place to escape, for a few minutes anyway, from the war that was going on outside.

The GIs were most appreciative that I had taken their wounded buddies to the MASH (I didn't mention the little problem I'd had). And, as we walked back out to the helicopter to leave, the sergeant in charge of the unit said, "You helicopter pilots and medics from the MASH are our heros, and frankly, if we didn't know you were there when we need you, I'm just not sure how many of us would be willing to do what we do."

I've always remembered what the sergeant said to me that day on a scarred Korean battlefield. It made me proud to be one of the "Battlefield Taxi" drivers. The three wounded men all recovered, and I submitted a recommendation for a Medal of Valor for my medic. I'm also proud, on this fiftieth anniversary of the Korean War, to have been a part of that unprecedented lifesaving effort.

5

Winged S

When the peace talks finally ended and the shooting stopped in Korea in 1953, I was sent home just in time for Christmas. It was great being with my family again in the good old USA. I was assigned as a helicopter pilot to the 43rd Air Rescue Squadron, 4th Air Rescue Group, at McChord Air Force Base in Washington, where I had flown my first helicopter.

A couple of weeks before Christmas 1955 my squadron commander called me into his office and told me that I had been selected to ferry one of our H-19 helicopters to the Sikorsky factory for modification. I was pleased at the assignment, because in those days we rarely had the opportunity to make such a long flight in the helicopter. It was approximately twenty-seven hundred miles from McChord Air Force Base to the factory in Stratford, Connecticut.

The down side was that it was winter, and the helicopter was not equipped to fly instruments. That meant I'd be delayed by storms, and it could take weeks to complete the trip.

"Sir, I've spent two of the last three Christmases away from my family. I hate to be gone again. Is there any possibility I can wait till after Christmas to make the flight?" I asked.

The major shook his head. "No. My orders are to get it there ASAP."

"ASAP?"

"That's correct."

I could see he wasn't going to bend on a delay, so I went to my second option. "I may have to take a circuitous route to avoid long delays because of weather."

The major looked at me suspiciously for a moment and then said, "Take whatever route is necessary, as long as it gets you there."

The weatherman had told me that I could skirt most of the winter weather by going south—deep south. And that's what I did. I flew the H-19 with my copilot, Lt. Bill Tuttle, and crew chief, T.Sgt. John Maddox, down the west coast of Washington, Oregon, and California. Then we went along the Mexican border of Arizona, New Mexico, and Texas, to the gulf coast, across Florida, and then up the Atlantic coast to the Sikorsky plant in Stratford, arriving three days before Christmas. We had airline reservations for home the next day.

There was a welcoming committee with a big surprise for us at the Sikorsky factory. One of them was a smiling gentleman wearing a black fedora. It was Igor Ivanovich Sikorsky, one of the greatest aeronautical engineers and designers of all time. He had been one of my aviation heros for many years, so it was a genuine thrill and an honor to meet him. He bowed slightly and shook my hand firmly when we were introduced. "Congratulations, Captain Kirkland, on your record-breaking flight," he said.

"My record-breaking flight?" I sort of croaked, uncertain of what he meant.

He was still smiling, his dark, thin mustache turned up at the corners of his mouth. "Yes. Didn't you know?"

I shook my head.

"Your flight of approximately seven thousand miles breaks all helicopter distance records to date that we know of," said one of the other Sikorsky officials standing there.

I found out later the information on our route across the continent came from my daily flight reports to headquarters. But at the time, I had no idea we had broken a distance record. I glanced at my crew, and we all smiled and tried to look like record breakers. Actually, we were too embarrassed to admit that all we'd done was circumnavigate the bad weather so we could get home for Christmas.

"Come gentlemen, we have some refreshments waiting," said one of the others in the welcoming committee.

We were escorted inside the factory to a conference room where there were soft drinks, coffee, and cake.

"What type of problems did you encounter on such a long flight?" asked Sikorsky, as soon as we were seated around the table with our refreshments. I could tell from the way he asked the question that he was genuinely interested in my answer.

We'd had a couple of small problems, which I described for him, like an un-

Author (left), copilot Lt. Bill Tuttle, and T.Sgt. John Maddox shortly after arrival at the Sikorsky factory at the completion of a record-breaking flight in the Sikorsky H-19, December 1955.

scheduled landing in a cornfield when the throttle bellcrank sheered. That excited him, and he wanted to know exactly what happened and how we repaired it.

What a fascinating experience it was to be sitting there discussing helicopters with one of the great men of aviation and the man most of the helicopter world considered the father of the helicopter.

Born in Kiev, Russia, on May 25, 1889, Igor Sikorsky decided early that aviation was the love of his life, and vertical flight the passion of that love. His first efforts included a helicopter he designed and built himself when he was nineteen years old. It had a wooden frame and crude rotor blades that were powered by a 25-horsepower Anzani engine. In the backyard of the Sikorsky home on a spring day in 1910, the engine roared and the rotor blades whirled, with Sikorsky at the controls. But all that rose from the earth was a lot of dust.

Despite the failure of his first helicopter, Sikorsky told his father he was certain he could design a helicopter that would fly. But he turned his attention to conventional aviation and within a year had designed and built an airplane with the help of schoolmates from the polytechnic institute he attended. He taught himself to fly the plane and set several world records.

Within two years he had designed and produced six successful airplanes and, after that, the world's first four-engine airplane, the Grand, which also set numerous world records. After the Grand's success, Sikorsky was widely acclaimed in Russia, and personally honored by Czar Nicholas.

But the Bolshevik Revolution forced Sikorsky to flee his homeland and immigrate to America in 1919. His arrival in New York went unnoticed, and he struggled to make ends meet for several years. Then, with the help of a few friends, and parts from a junkyard, he designed, built, and flew his first American aircraft on a Long Island chicken farm in early 1923.

He formed the Sikorsky Aero Engineering Corporation a short time later, moved to nearby Roosevelt Field, and began to design a family of amphibians that would soon make aviation history. His twin-engine, eight-passenger S-38 amphibian was used to pioneer air routes throughout South America, the Hawaiian Islands, and other remote corners of the world.

In 1929 Sikorsky moved his company to Connecticut and became a division of United Aircraft Corporation. There, he met and worked with Charles Lindbergh, and together they ushered in the era of the Pan American Clipper ships that linked the Americas. Sikorsky's next amphibian, the huge S-40, four-engine flying boats crossed both oceans and carried passengers to the ends of the world.

Throughout the 1930s Sikorsky quietly turned his attention back to his long-held passion for the helicopter. How he convinced management at United Aircraft to allow him to proceed with a helicopter experimental project in 1938, when the depression was causing severe reductions, is a story in itself. It was reported that Sikorsky's rationale to Don Brown, the chief executive at United Aircraft, went something like this:

I believe the time has come when we need to go ahead with vertical lift. To design and build a successful helicopter will require a most serious effort, demanding something more than just reason. It will require intuitive engineering and creative faith, which I believe we possess in our company.

The development of a helicopter is so important to the future of aviation and society, that it becomes our inherent responsibility to understand and pursue it. Admittedly, it is radical, but the helicopter concept is wholly rational, and, like no other vehicle, it will operate without regard to prepared landing surfaces. Therefore it will free us of the serious handicap of airport limitations imposed by fixed-wing aircraft.

Now the helicopter is not competitive with the airplane. It is complementary, and I envision it will bring into the world a whole new means of saving lives.

Don Brown was apparently convinced and gave the green light for the production of the first experimental helicopter, which was to be known as the VS-300 [Vought-Sikorsky experimental aircraft number 300]. A happy Sikorsky returned, after a thirty-year absence, to his first love.

Years later Sikorsky described his thinking when he and his small crew began work on the VS-300. It went something like this:

We knew what we were doing, but we also knew our first guess would not be our last one, so I deliberately made the helicopter more or less as a contraption so we could adjust, remove, or add, as we needed. We could have ordered castings and forgings and specially built gears, etc., but I wanted none of that. The ship would have a welded tube frame and belts for quickly changing the ratio of rotor speed, and we used gears from a Mack truck.

His comments on first flight: "In September of 1938, five months after we started, our machine was ready for first flight. It wasn't much of a flight, but it was better than my first attempt in 1910. It was very difficult to control, but I got the VS-300 four to six inches off the ground for about ten seconds. We considered that a great beginning."

On his learning to fly the VS-300:

It was equivalent to riding a bucking horse, with little positive control. But over a period of several months we made numerous changes in the control system in our search

Igor Sikorsky, flying his VS-300, lifts off into aviation history, September 14, 1939. (Courtesy Helicopter Foundation International)

for stability and control, including the use of auxiliary rotors. Finally, we got it to the point that I could keep it under reasonable control. But I was somewhat restricted because management insisted I remain in tethered flight, so that if I crashed it would be localized. Then one day when the machine yanked the chain right out of the concrete, I declared we were free of our shackles. Besides, I reasoned, the danger is not in flying through the air but in striking the ground. Hereafter, I was permitted to seek safety in free flight.

Eugene Wilson, senior vice president of United Aircraft, described his impression of watching Sikorsky in one of those early flights in an article in *Reader's Digest* [Eugene E. Wilson, "The Most Unforgettable Character I've Met," December 1956]: "He (Igor) sat there in his business suit and prim fedora on the 'front porch' of his crazy looking craft, looking like a baffled professor trying to remember his notes, and I marveled that he ever learned to fly the thing."

On May 6, 1941, Sikorsky established a new helicopter world record for endurance by remaining airborne in his VS-300 for one hour, thirty-three minutes, and twenty-six seconds. Within a month, United Aircraft received its first government contract for a Sikorsky helicopter, and America's helicopter industry was born.

As we sat there sipping coffee and eating cake, Sikorsky seemed so down to earth, I had the feeling that I could ask him the question that had been on my mind for many years. So I did.

"Mr. Sikorsky, is it true that the VS-300 would climb vertical, fly sideward, and backward, but wouldn't go forward?"

He smiled broadly. "So, you have heard that story?"

I returned the smile and admitted that I had.

"Well, after I had demonstrated the craft to our senior management a couple of times, the president at that time, Mr. Eugene Wilson, said to me, 'Igor, you have shown us a ship hovering over one spot, flying sideways and rearward, but it occurs to me that I have not seen it flying forward. Why is that?' I replied, 'Mr. Wilson, that is a secondary engineering problem which we haven't solved yet.'

"Frankly, captain, I was getting desperate over that problem, because I could make the machine do everything but go forward. I had about decided to simply turn the seat around and then backward would be forward. But the problem then would be that it wouldn't fly backward, so we had no choice but to solve the problem, which we did by replacing the two rotors with one single center rotor and use cyclic pitch control for stability.

"But there were an awful lot of similar problems which we also solved over a period of time, and now we have helicopters that can do what you just did, captain, fly seven thousand miles without a major mishap or delay, and can do the important thing I always envisioned the helicopter would: save lives."

"Yes, sir, that they can do. I know."

He looked at me for a moment. "You were in Korea, captain?"

I nodded.

"Then you wear the Winged S."

I nodded again.

The "Winged S" was the trademark of Sikorsky aircraft. It was also a prestigious gold lapel pen, which Sikorsky initiated and awarded to pilots and crew of a Sikorsky helicopter who had saved a life. I earned mine in Korea, flying a Sikorsky H-5. It flew forward right well.

6

Whirly-Girl One

Henrich Focke looked across the table at his chief test pilot, Ewald Rohlfs, and said, "Somehow we've got to get some attention at the top."

"I can't imagine how we could get any more attention than having just broken practically every helicopter-performance record on the books," growled Rohlfs.

Focke nodded. "I know, I know. You did a magnificent job with the Fa-61, Ewald. We got some good publicity all right, particularly after breaking the French records the Breguet-Dorand machine set last summer. But I still can't even get an appointment to see the procurement officials about a contract. They just aren't interested in our helicopter."

"Let's face it, Henrich, you're not going to get an appointment either. You're still in disfavor with the Nazis because you criticized them when you were at Focke-Wulf Aircraft," said the test pilot, sitting at a table with Focke at a local hofbrau.

Focke sighed and shook his head. "I'm afraid you're right, Ewald."

The two men took a sip of their drinks and were silent for a moment. "The Fa-61 is a great step forward in rotary-wing development, Henrich," Rohlfs suddenly blurted. "So don't despair, something will turn up."

The petite, pretty young woman stepped up next to the Fa-16 helicopter, and surveyed it with sparkling eyes. "What a fascinating machine, Herr Focke!" she exclaimed.

"Thank you, Fräulein Reitsch," said the pleased aircraft designer. "Your reaction does not surprise me. Most pilots are something less than thrilled with its appearance, but someone with your experience and mechanical aptitude would quickly see the aerodynamic effectiveness of the design."

Hanna Reitsch smiled. "I'm afraid I must confess that I have little expertise in rotary-wing dynamics, Herr Focke. Frankly, what fascinates me about your machine is the challenge it presents."

A Luftwaffe colonel, wearing wings and standing next to Hanna, ran his eyes over the ungainly Fa-61. It had an open cockpit in a wingless, fabric-covered fuselage, with tricycle landing gear. Three-bladed rotors, which resembled giant fans, were mounted on skeletal outriggers on each side. The horizontal stabilizer was on top of the rudder instead of at the bottom, and the nose-mounted aircraft engine had a small stubby propeller. The colonel involuntarily grimaced, then recovering, glanced at Henrich Focke, and nodded discreetly.

Focke caught the nod and with a smile said, "Yes. My test pilot tells me it is a challenge to fly. But someone with your experience would have no problem, I'm sure. Uh . . . would you like to fly it, Fräulein?"

Hanna looked at Focke in surprise, then glanced at the colonel, who smiled and said, "The Führer himself wishes you to fly the Fa-61 helicopter, Fräulein Reitsch."

"I would love to fly it!" she said without hesitation.

After a date was set for the flight, and Reitsch and the Luftwaffe colonel had departed, Rohlfs said to Focke, "What was that all about?"

"It may be what we were waiting for," replied Focke.

"Why do you say that?"

"That colonel is on the general staff, and you heard what he said. The Führer himself requested that we let Fräulein Reitsch fly the Fa-61."

"I smell a rat. They never do anything unless it's to their advantage."

"True, but in this case it may serve our purpose, too. Hanna Reitsch is well known in the fatherland, and she got much publicity recently when the Führer made her an honorary Flugkapitan [flight captain]. She is the only female test pilot in the Luftwaffe, and when she flies the Fa-61, she will be the first woman in the world to fly a helicopter. That should get us some attention in the right place."

"Yeah, and what if she wrecks the machine?"

"She won't. She is an unusually talented and astute pilot with an instinctive understanding of flight parameters."

"Yes, I know. She started flying at an early age and has flown many aircraft in the Luftwaffe since. But she has never flown a helicopter, and that little beauty is not easy to fly, Henrich."

"A little male ego there, Ewald?"

The test pilot grinned. "Probably, but I don't want to see that bird wrecked. Since there is no such thing as dual instruction in the Fa-61, she's on her own. And if she gets hurt, you not only won't get any contracts, you'll probably have the SS at your door."

A frown passed over the designer's face, and he let out a sigh. "Well, we are committed now, so all we can do is hope that Hanna Reitsch is as good as they say she is."

It was an exciting new challenge for Hanna to fly Henrich Focke's Fa-61. However, she realized that it would not be easy. It was, in actuality, the world's first reliable helicopter, with its first flight only a year earlier in 1936. Therefore, there were no flight manuals and no how-to instructions. She would have to solo the machine with only Rohlfs's preflight coaching. Success would depend on her judgment and instincts. She had flown many dangerous test flights in fixed-wing aircraft, but she knew from her knowledge of aerodynamics that fixed wing and rotary wing were two different breeds.

On the appointed day, Reitsch, Focke, and Rohlfs met on the small field where she was to attempt her first flight. Reitsch had predetermined that she would take the challenge of helicopter flight in the same manner she had taken all her previous test-flying challenges—with excited anticipation, but with caution and intense concentration on the mechanical and aerodynamic reactions to control applications.

Reitsch listened intently to Rohlfs's explanation of the principal dynamics of the Fa-61 and how to maintain flight control:

> The rotors on the outriggers are powered by the nose-mounted, 160-horsepower aircraft engine. The propeller also provides engine cooling. By moving the control stick forward and backward, you can tilt the rotors forward and backward together, and keep the nose from going up and down, while managing climb and descent. By moving the stick sideways, you can increase the pitch of the blades of one rotor and reduce it on the other to control the roll. By applying rudder pedal, you can tilt the two rotors forward and backward in opposite directions, to control yaw.

Reitsch concentrated a moment, then repeated Rohlfs's instructions verbatim.

Rohlfs nodded. "Any questions?"

Hanna smiled. "I'm sure there will be, Ewald. But first, I'd like some hands-on application."

As Rohlfs watched Hanna climb into the helicopter's open cockpit, he couldn't help wonder how a five-foot, ninety-pound woman could possibly handle the control forces she would have while maneuvering the Fa-61.

It wasn't easy. But after sitting in the cockpit for hours (on cushions for height), studying the engine and control levers, then working the controls with the engine running and rotors turning at low RPM, she was finally ready. Hanna revved the engine to full power and herded Henrich Focke's Fa-61 helicopter off the ground to became the world's first female helicopter pilot—"Whirly-Girl Number One."

"Come in, colonel, and have a chair," said a smiling Henrich Focke, quickly getting to his feet as the Luftwaffe officer walked into the small, cluttered office. "It's a pleasure to see you again. Could I get you something to drink?"

"No thank you, Herr Focke," replied the colonel, seating himself and removing a silver cigarette case from an inside-blouse pocket. "I have asked that Fräulein Reitsch join us, but I wanted a moment with you first."

"Yes, sir?"

"The Führer is pleased to hear that Fräulein Reitsch has soloed the helicopter," said the colonel, lighting a cigarette.

Focke nodded. "I'm glad the Führer is pleased. Fräulein Reitsch is an outstanding pilot and doing well in the Fa-61."

The colonel nodded. "Yes, I'm sure she is. But I want to know if she is now competent in the machine?"

"Yes, I believe she is."

"You believe? Is she or isn't she?" snapped the colonel, blowing out a column of smoke.

The aircraft designer cleared his throat, "In my opinion, she is competent."

The colonel nodded. "This could be important for you, Herr Focke . . . very important. Do I make myself clear?"

"Yes, colonel. I understand and . . . Oh, come in Fräulein Reitsch," said Focke as Hanna appeared at the door.

After Hanna had seated herself, she and Focke looked at the colonel expectantly. He leaned forward, focusing on her, and said, "The Führer sends his congratulations, Fräulein Reitsch, on your achievement of becoming the world's first female helicopter pilot."

Hanna Reitsch flying Henrich Focke's Fa-61 helicopter, practicing for her publicity performance in the Deutschlandhalle sports arena, Berlin, February 1938.

"Thank you, colonel. I'm grateful to the Führer for the opportunity. The Fa-61 helicopter is a marvelous flying machine. Herr Focke has made a major contribution to the advancement of aviation."

The Luftwaffe officer nodded, took a puff of his cigarette, and said, "Now I have a question for you, Fräulein Reitsch. Herr Focke tells me you are proficient in the machine. Are you?"

Reitsch glanced at Focke. They had become friends during the period of her transition flying in the Fa-61, and she didn't want to embarrass him. But in fact, she did feel competent, so she turned to the colonel and said, "Herr Focke is correct. I am proficient in the machine."

"Good, because you are scheduled to demonstrate the helicopter next week, a special demonstration of great importance to the Führer and to the Third Reich."

"I would be honored," Reitsch quickly said.

"Your demonstration could have a far-reaching effect, since you will be performing for one of the most influential men in the aviation world—the American, Charles A. Lindbergh."

The Luftwaffe colonel was correct. It was no secret in diplomatic circles that Lindbergh was on a tour of Nazi Germany to assess its airpower. Adolph Hitler and the Nazis were anxious to impress him. And they did.

Reitsch's 1938 flight demonstration of the Fa-61 was so impressive, Lindbergh told the international press that it was the most striking aeronautical development he had ever seen. Shortly after her demonstration to Lindbergh, Reitsch took the Fa-61 on a publicity tour across Germany, and, in the process, broke a number of Rohlfs's records. Then, in February 1938, she scored her supreme publicity coup by demonstrating the helicopter inside Berlin's cavernous Deutschlandhalle sports arena.

Every night for three weeks, during performances at a trade show, she put the Fa-61 through its paces with vertical, side, and backward flight, which, of course, had never been seen before. Despite the aerodynamic idiosyncracies and control forces prevalent in that primitive technology, Reitsch had mastered the technique of flying the machine so thoroughly that she made it look easy to the throngs of spectators who came to see the demonstrations.

Newsreels and photographs of her performance appeared around the world, and, shortly afterward, Focke received a contract for an enlarged version of the Fa-61, and then an even larger model, the Fa-223.

Hanna Reitsch continued test-pilot flying and flew virtually every aircraft in the Luftwaffe, including the early jet fighters, the V-1 "Flying Bomb," and the unstable Me 163B rocket plane. She was the only woman ever to be awarded Germany's Iron Cross First Class.

Whirly-Girls is an international association of female helicopter pilots organized by Jean Ross Howard (#13) in 1955. Currently, it has a membership of over 1,115 members from 32 countries.

The dialog is, of course, my imagination. But it was based on historical records and my own personal conversation with Hanna Reitsch, who I had the pleasure of meeting at the Helicopter Association of America convention in 1976. I asked her, What aircraft did she consider her favorite? She smiled and admitted that she enjoyed helicopter flying very much. I sort of suspected that would be the answer from "Whirly-Girl One."

7

Sky Knight

Capt. Hugh McDonald of the Los Angeles County Sheriff's Office walked slowly around the helicopter, examining it as though it was a questionable piece of evidence at a crime scene. As a bureau chief of one of the largest law enforcement agencies in the world, McDonald had a critical eye and, in this instance, did not like what he saw.

"It doesn't look very substantial," he blurted, halting in front of the plastic nose bubble of the Hughes 269 and directing his piercing eyes to the pilot, Bill Wyatt, who stood nervously watching him.

Turning on a smile, the pilot replied, "Well, you know the old saying, Chief: the best things often come in small packages."

Wyatt laughed at his analogy. McDonald didn't.

Wyatt, a born salesman with a warm, congenial personality, kept his smile and looked at McDonald, a big, bull-necked man, who towered over him. "You see, chief, this little bird was designed small but tough and dependable, like the venerable Jeep. In fact we call it the 'Flying Jeep.' Its secret is its simplicity of design. The elimination of heavy, complex hardware makes it light and dependable. It has a proven Lycoming engine that runs a simple belt-drive system with a ring-and-pinion transmission. The tail cone is simply a piece of extruded aluminum and the rotor blades are bonded aluminum. This little bird is so high performing, it only needs a twenty-six-foot rotor system, which means it can get in and out of small places. Why this helicopter can—"

"Yeah, yeah, whatever. I told Sheriff Pitchess I'd give it a try, and, since we're desperate, let's get on with it."

"Yes, sir. Just climb right up there into the seat, and we'll be on our way in a minute," said Wyatt.

When McDonald had pulled his tall frame into the bubble and fastened the seat belt, Wyatt handed him a handi-talkie police radio. He then snapped on his flashlight and made one last check around the helicopter where it sat on the darkened ramp at the Hughes Aircraft Company Airport, in Culver City, California. He directed the flashlight beam over the critical areas as he walked around the aircraft: rotor blade tie downs removed, gas cap secure, pitot cover off, no evident damage. Everything appeared in order.

Wyatt reached for the pilot's door handle, hesitated, and glanced toward the east. Even though it was several miles to the city of Watts, he could see the red glow of the raging fires reflecting off the layer of smog that hung low over the Los Angeles basin on this hot August night in 1965. He wouldn't have any trouble finding his destination, went a thought. But then what? What could a lone helicopter do over a burning city? Well, it could do what he'd told the sheriff it could, and this was his chance to prove it. So just get in the helicopter and go, Wyatt.

As the manager of fleet sales for the Aircraft Division of the Hughes Tool Company, Wyatt had been trying for months to get the Los Angeles law enforcement community interested in the helicopter as a sort of flying patrol car. He had convinced himself that it would work, but he had not been able to convince many others. Now he had an unexpected opportunity to show, in a high-visibility way, what the helicopter could do under adverse conditions. He had called the sheriff's office and made the offer right after the Watts riots had broken out, but was told they were too busy to bother with a helicopter. Then the rioting and burning had become so violent and widespread that command and control had all but collapsed. Sheriff Peter Pitchess decided to try the helicopter, and Wyatt was finally on base with his model 269 "Flying Jeep."

Within a few minutes Wyatt took off from the Hughes Airport, and headed east, with the flames from the fires plainly visible across the horizon.

"My God, look at that!" bellowed McDonald.

"It looks like the whole city is on fire," replied Wyatt, watching the leaping flames from burning buildings shooting up like erupting volcanos, spewing showers of flaming sparks and boiling clouds of smoke into the night sky. Some of the fires shot so high overhead, they caused eerie reflections of dancing shapes of red and red orange mixing with the dull grays of the low-hanging, smog-filled overcast.

As the helicopter approached the burning city, Wyatt circled around to the upwind side of the flames and smoke. Although visibility was limited, he was still able to give McDonald a bird's-eye view of the scene below. It looked like a World War II film of a devastated European city after a night-bombing raid. But those films were taken from thousands of feet up. This scene was from five hundred feet where details were strikingly visible.

"Look! Look!" shouted McDonald. "I can see people running and . . . There! Did you see that? That guy threw a firebomb into a store! Jesus!" The captain grabbed his portable radio.

"Command, this is McDonald, do you copy?"

No answer.

McDonald repeated his call.

"Mac, is that you?"

"Yeah! Yeah! It's me. Is that you, sheriff?"

"This is Sheriff Pitchess. I can't read you very well, Mac. What's that noise?"

"I'm in the helicopter, sheriff."

"You are? Where are you?"

"I'm flying over the city, and you wouldn't believe what I can see."

"You're over the city?"

"Yeah."

"Watch out for gunfire! There're snipers in every quadrant."

"I know. I can see them down there."

"You can see them?"

"I can see everything, sheriff. I can see the snipers, the firebombers, the looters, the fires. All of it, including a burning, overturned police car and an abandoned fire truck."

"All right! Our command structure is in serious trouble and communications are in shambles. Because of gunfire we've had to pull back, and we've got both fire and police units trapped in there. "It looks like that whirlybird is gonna have to be our eye in the sky, Mac."

And so it was that night, the next day, and several days and nights to follow that the helicopter acted as an observation and command post for the Los Angeles County Sheriff's Office and the other law enforcement and fire fighting agencies involved in the 1965 riots in the city of Watts, California.

This was the first significant use of a helicopter for this type of aerial law enforcement in the United States, and it established the basis for the future application of helicopters as airborne patrol cars in both day and night operations. That first application was, of course, primitive by today's standards, but it opened eyes, and doors, to the potential.

Based on the helicopter experiences during the Watts riots, the Los Angeles County Sheriff's Office and the city of Lakewood, California, applied for a Federal Law Enforcement Assistance Act grant to conduct an eighteen-month study of the effectiveness of day-and-night helicopter patrol for crime suppression. The grant was approved and the mayor of Lakewood, George Nye, headed a group of mayors from neighboring cities to support the program. A day-to-day evaluation of its effectiveness was conducted by Dr. Robert Gutherie of the Department of Criminology at Long Beach State College.

The world's first day-and-night airborne helicopter patrol, named "Sky Knight," was initiated on June 6, 1966. Hughes 269 helicopters, flown by sheriff's deputies, functioned as airborne patrol cars, flying around the clock, as an adjunct to their counterparts on the streets below. At the completion of the project, Gutherie's final report confirmed that day-and-night helicopter patrol over an urban area was a highly effective tool for crime suppression and rapid response, when used in conjunction with a ground patrol car.

Armed with the results of the Lakewood project, Wyatt was now ready to take on the challenge of convincing city and county law enforcement agencies across the country to initiate airborne patrol to reduce crime in their jurisdictions. His first stop was the office of his supervisor, Hughes director of sales, Jud Brandreth.

"Boss, we got the final report on Sky Knight, and it proves conclusively that our little helicopter is an effective tool as an airborne patrol car."

"That's great, Bill. What's your plan?"

"Well, I'd like to start off by hiring Chief Hugh McDonald as a consultant."

"Hugh McDonald? I didn't think he was all that thrilled with our 269 helicopter."

Wyatt grinned. "He wasn't at first. But he's a believer now and so convinced of the concept that I'm sure he would work with us on the program. He's retiring from the sheriff's office this month, and, since he's well known in law enforcement circles, he would be a great asset to our program."

Brandreth leaned back in his chair and nodded. "Okay. Have you worked up a budget?"

Wyatt shifted in his chair. "Yeah. . . . What I got in mind is having a seminar for our field salesman so that McDonald can teach them the concept. He would provide the expertise in law enforcement and design the sales data aimed at law

This publicity photograph shows the concept of the airborne patrol helicopter working with its ground-unit partner in the Los Angles County Sheriff's Sky Knight project, June 1966.

enforcement agencies. We would use the Sky Knight data, of course, as support for the concept. Then our field salesmen would go out and do the footwork, calling on city and county agencies, and demonstrating how the helicopter works on police patrol."

Brandreth nodded. "Sounds good. What's it gonna cost me?"

Wyatt shifted in his chair again and handed Brandreth a folder. "These are preliminary figures. I'll hone them down some later."

Brandreth opened the folder and glanced at the numbers, folded it and handed it back to Wyatt. "What did your wife put in your breakfast cereal this morning, Bill?"

Wyatt grinned. "I don't know. Must have been pretty potent stuff, huh?"

"Too potent for me."

"Elizabeth took a gamble."

"They were her jewels to gamble. All the jewels around here belong to Howard Hughes."

"Actually boss, there isn't much of a gamble. This is a sure thing if I've ever seen one. Sky Knight proved that the helicopter can be an effective tool for law enforcement. All we got to do is spread the word."

As I said earlier in the story, Bill Wyatt was a natural-born salesman, and he convinced Brandreth to fund the law enforcement program. As it turned out over the years, Wyatt was right, and today nearly every major law enforcement agency in the country operates helicopters—all makes and models. But it didn't come easily, and Wyatt wasn't the only sales manager who had to convince his boss of the role helicopters would play in law enforcement. It required many years of dedicated and expensive efforts by not only Hughes, but most of the other helicopter manufacturers, including Agusta, Bell, Brantly, Enstrom, Eurocopters, Hiller, Robinson, Schweizer, Sikorsky, and others.

My part in that long effort began in late 1967. I was the midwest Hughes salesman stationed in Chicago, when Wyatt and McDonald flew out from Los Angeles to talk to me about the law enforcement program. Our meeting went something like this:

"As you know, Richard, we have launched our law enforcement sales program with Chief McDonald's help, and we have convinced some cities in the Los Angeles area to adopt the Sky Knight system. But as you also know, we haven't had much luck in the midwest or east yet. You got any ideas on that?" asked Wyatt, who was now the national sales manager and my supervisor.

We were in a little restaurant on State Street, in the windy city, and the waitress had just arrived with our lunch, which gave me a chance to think about how I was going to answer Wyatt's question. He was a great guy and a super boss, so I knew I could tell it the way it was, but I didn't want to sound negative.

"Here's to the future of the flying patrol car," said McDonald, holding up his glass of iced tea. Wyatt looked at me and winked. The chief had become an enthusiastic supporter of the Sky Knight concept.

"I'll drink to that," I said, picking up my glass. "But I have to tell you fellows that the cops out here in the midwest and east all say that it might work in California, but it won't out here."

"Why not?" asked McDonald with furrowed eyebrows.

"Because they say that in California the streets are paved with gold and lined with rose bushes . . . and the weather is mostly blue sky."

Wyatt laughed.

"That's a bunch of shit," growled McDonald.

"I know it is, chief," I said. "But that's the perception."

"I don't know where all that gold was when I was trying to get funding to start this whole thing," said Wyatt.

"Got any ideas, Richard?" asked McDonald.

I nodded. "We gotta pick a city out here, zero in on it, and convince them that helicopters will work here the same as they did out west."

We all took a bite of our lunches.

"You got someplace in mind?" asked Wyatt.

"Yeah, I do. Kansas City, Missouri."

McDonald nodded. "Good old Kansas City, part east and part west. Good choice."

"Yeah. It's in the Show Me State. If we could prove the Sky Knight concept works there, the rest of the country would accept it," agreed Wyatt.

I nodded. "My thoughts exactly. . . . And having 316 square miles makes it one of the largest cities in the United States."

"I didn't realize it was that big," said Wyatt. "You're gonna need some help."

"I got something in mind on that, too. I met a sharp, ex-Vietnam helicopter pilot down there recently, Donald Bachali. He would be a great asset to the program."

"Okay. Is hc available?"

"No."

Wyatt looked at me questioningly.

"I mean he's an architect," I explained. "But I'm gonna talk him into becoming a helicopter salesman."

Wyatt grinned, "I like your style, Richard."

Wyatt gave me a green light, and I flew to Kansas City and hired me a sales partner. I didn't have to talk real hard because Bachali loved helicopters. He was also another natural salesman, with a warm smile and a sincerity that eventually made him the company's top law enforcement salesman.

I had designed a plan of action to convince the folks in Kansas City that utilizing the helicopter as an airborne patrol car would reduce crime. Now the challenge was to figure out a way to get the police department interested enough to listen to what I had to say. I got some help in an unforeseen way.

When I explained the problem to Bachali, my new sales assistant, he quickly said, "Hey, one of my old school buddies, Bill Ellingsworth, is the police reporter for the Kansas City *Star* newspaper. Bill has a good relationship with the chief of police, Clarence Kelly. Maybe he could help us."

"I knew you were gonna do well at this job, Don. Call up Bill and see if he can meet us for dinner."

Bachali made the call, and, sure enough, his friend met us that evening at the grand old Muehlebach Hotel. Bill Ellingsworth was a sharp, young newspaper reporter who quickly picked up on the concept. But when I asked him his thoughts on how to approach the chief of police, he grimaced and said, "That's gonna be a tough one, Richard. Chief Kelly is a super guy, and a good, forward-thinking chief. But he doesn't like flying machines of any kind."

"You're kidding?" I groaned.

Ellingsworth shook his head. "I don't think there is any way you're gonna interest him in a flying patrol car."

I could see my plans for a Sky Knight program in Kansas City going up in smoke. I had discovered early in my sales career that if the boss was not on your team, you were whistling dixie.

"Any suggestions, Bill?" asked Bachali.

Ellingsworth let out a big sigh and thought for a moment. "Well, he does like publicity, he knows it's important. Tell you what, I'll see if I can get my editor at the *Star* to do a feature on your helicopter, and, maybe, we could get him in the act for some pictures. That way you will at least have a chance to show him the helicopter."

"You're on," I said feeling now that at least we had a shot at a program in Kansas City.

A couple weeks later Ellingsworth got the green light from his editor, and Chief Kelly accepted an invitation to a press conference and photo op. Don and I flew a new Sky Knight helicopter into town and landed on a grassy knoll right there in the city, a short distance from the famous Hereford Cow statue. Anybody who has ever been to Kansas City knows where that is.

Bill Ellingsworth was there with a *Star* photographer, and we all stood around at the appointed time, waiting nervously for Chief Kelly to show.

"You think he might not come?" I asked.

"Oh, he'll be here. He always keeps his appointments. I'm just not sure how long he'll stay," said Ellingsworth.

About that time a police cruiser pulled up, and Chief Clarence Kelly stepped out of the backseat. He was a big man with broad shoulders and gray hair. Ellingsworth introduced him to Bachali and me, and he shook our hands with a firm grip.

"Chief, let me briefly show you this new-technology helicopter that was so successful in the police Sky Knight program in California," I quickly said.

"I read about that," he replied, adjusting his glasses and looking at the 269.

I waved my arm for him to come closer to the bird, but he ignored me, standing his ground there beside the police cruiser. So I pointed at some of the features of the helicopter as I described them.

He seemed interested, but wary. Fortunately, Ellingsworth intervened. "Chief, could I get you to move over next to the helicopter so we could get some pictures?"

The chief nodded and stepped closer. Then, after shooting several pictures, the photographer said, "Chief, would you mind climbing up into the seat for just a couple of shots?"

Ellingsworth and I exchanged glances and held our breath, because it looked like he was going to turn around and leave. But after a hesitation, he surprisingly agreed. I showed him how to get into the cockpit, then ran around and climbed into the other seat beside him and quickly began to explain how the helicopter functioned, while the *Star* photographer snapped pictures.

Then came my big break when the photographer said, "Mr. Kirkland, would you mind starting up the windmill on top. That would make a great shot."

I didn't even look at the chief. I just shouted, "Clear!" and hit the starter button. That little HIO 360 engine roared to life on the first crank, and within a couple of minutes I had the rotors turning. When I looked across at Chief Kelly, he was pale and staring straight ahead. But I figured I was committed now and it couldn't be any worse than it already was, so I went for broke. I reached across and fastened his seat belt and slipped the headset on him, while the Kansas City *Star* photographer ran around the helicopter getting pictures from all angles.

"Chief, as long as we got her going, I'll just take you for a short spin, so you can see how this little baby works," I said on the intercom, and pulled pitch.

That was almost thirty five-years ago, but I can still see, as though it happened yesterday, the fear on Kelly's face and his white knuckles gripping the side of the helicopter.

I lifted the 269 to a hover, and gently moved off the knoll and over the top of the Hereford Cow statue and some adjacent buildings. As we hovered along, I talked to him on the intercom calmly, pointing out the unique observation that is possible from the helicopter. "Look how clearly you can see objects below, chief. And how easily I can direct the helicopter in whatever direction I want to go. Look at that man down there. You can tell what color clothes he's wearing. And see how easily and quickly you can scan the top of that building." I glanced at Kelly. Perspiration streamed down his face, and he looked like he was going to explode, so I eased the bird around, slipped back over the grassy knoll, and landed.

He tore off the headset and found the door latch but could not get out because his safety belt was still fastened. I opened it for him, and he leaped out of the helicopter, hurried over to the cruiser, and sped away. When I shut down and crawled out of the helicopter, I was met with long faces.

"Jesus, what did he say?" asked Don anxiously.

"Nothing. He didn't say anything," I groaned.

"He's pissed," said the photographer.

"You can say that again," confirmed Ellingsworth.

"Well, I figured no guts no glory. And it's no glory and no sale," I lamented. "But we gave it our best shot fellows."

"Too bad," said Ellingsworth.

We all stood there a couple minutes and Ellingsworth said, "Well, there's a neat little bar just around the corner. We might as well go drown our sorrows in a mug of beer."

"Sounds like the thing to do," said Bachali.

Since I had to fly the bird off the grassy knoll, I was restricted to coke, but the others had a couple of cold beers. We ate some sandwiches and potato chips as we hashed over our disaster.

"I hope you don't get into trouble with your editor," I said to Bill.

"I don't know just what to think. That isn't like Chief Kelly to just walk away without a word. But then, like I told you, Richard, he hates flying."

"Yeah, he was really upset," said the photographer.

"I guess I blew it," I had to admit.

After we had hashed it over a dozen times and finished our lunch, I decided there was nothing to do now but crawl in the helicopter and get out of Dodge. Bill drove us back to the knoll, and we were standing around on the grass when a police car came speeding up and slid to a stop.

"Looks like he's gonna throw us all in jail," I groaned.

"You really think so?" said Don, as we watched a sergeant jump out of the car and pull open the backdoor.

Chief Kelly stepped out and walked briskly across the grass to where I stood. "Yeah. I'm sure of it," I mumbled.

"Mr. Kirkland, I apologize for my abrupt behavior earlier. But I've never liked flying, and I was rather shocked to suddenly find myself airborne." He turned and looked at the helicopter. "But that is an amazing machine, and I want you to take me up in it again."

I stared at him, without comprehension. "What?"

"I'd like you to fly me again, Mr. Kirkland."

Comprehension returned. "Yes, sir!" I blurted.

A big smile blossomed on Ellingsworth; the photographer sprang into action and Bachali ran over and opened the 269 door for the chief.

It took me a minute or two to regain my sales composure, then I settled down and explained the operation of the helicopter and all its unique qualities. The chief, although nervous at first, also settled down after a few minutes and listened intently, asking astute questions. Then we lifted off the grassy knoll gently and flew over the Hereford Cow. Our fight around Kansas City went something like this:

"The ideal altitude for the airborne patrol car is five hundred feet. From there you have ample height to effect an autorotation in the event of an emergency, and it is the optimum height to see and be seen as a deterrent to crime in the streets."

"Serving the same function as the patrol car in the street," observed Kelly.

"That's correct, sir. But the airborne patrol car can see much more than the ground patrol car in the traffic-clogged streets, and can be seen by many more people as a deterrent to crime in the streets."

"Yes, I can see that," he said, looking out at the city from our perch, as we flew above the streets and buildings.

"And we found in the Sky Knight project that the helicopter can maintain that same deterrent factor while patrolling thirty-five times more area than the ground unit in the same period of time."

Kelly looked across at me. "You mean the helicopter can cover thirty-five square miles while the ground unit is covering only one square mile?"

"That is correct, sir. And while on patrol, the helicopter can respond to a call for assistance five times faster than the ground unit, on average."

Kelly nodded. "But then what can he do when he flies to the crime scene?"

"The airborne patrol car then has complete control of the situation, because the observer can see everything that's going on. He can direct the ground units by radio, rendering escape of a suspect, or a suspect vehicle, all but impossible."

"I had no idea. . . ." muttered Kelly.

"Let's assume that blue car down there is a suspect. Watch how I can hover-fly above and behind him, and keep him in sight no matter where he goes," I said, following the blue car as it wove through traffic, stopping when he did for a traffic light, then continuing on. "Or, if you have a description of the suspect's car, and you want to see if it might be in that big parking lot down there. We'll just stop here a second," I said, bringing the bird to a hover over the lot. "And within a few seconds I can see there are two blue sedans down there. It would take some time for a ground unit to comb that lot and find those cars."

Kelly nodded. "I can see this will be a bonanza for spotting stolen vehicles."

"That it is. And if the dispatcher should tell us that a robbery is in progress at that bank down there, we can observe the entire facility from our perch here, and direct ground units into the proper position to apprehend any suspect, whether on foot or in a vehicle."

"Now, let's assume we just got an assault call on the other side of town," I said, pulling in full power and heading across the city. After a few minutes I spotted a park, and went down on the collective and set up a steep approach. "The helicopter does its best work in the air, observing and directing the ground units. But when necessary, it can land almost anywhere safely. Let's say we have a critical situation down there and the ground unit is not readily available."

I picked a spot where no one was around and came down between the trees, settling softly into the thick grass in the park. I could tell the chief was impressed.

"I can tell you, Mr. Kirkland, this machine is amazing. And what's even more amazing is that I'm not as apprehensive as I usually am when I have to fly. Frankly, I hate flying. But I swear, this is different."

I was ecstatic. I could tell that the chief was getting on my team. "It is unique, sir. And its new-technology design makes it actually safer than an automobile."

"What about at night? What do you do then?"

"Actually, it does its best work at night."

"Oh?"

"In order to show you, I'll have to give you a night demonstration, chief. But that handle there in front of you controls a powerful set of search lights that turns night into day, allowing the helicopter crew to check out rooftops, backyards, and dark alleys in a few seconds, which is not only effective and time saving, but eliminates that highly dangerous requirement for ground units. Dr. Gutherie stated in his final report that Sky Knight offers greatly increased officer safety in those types of high-risk night patrol operations."

I revved up to full RPM and eased the 269 up through the trees and headed across the city, continuing my presentation. "The airborne patrol car is also very effective against assaults and rapes in public parks at night, by merely flying over occasionally and flashing the light around. And it saved hundreds of thousands of dollars in reduction of night vandalism at schools and public buildings during the Sky Knight project. It's also effective in crowd control and civil disturbances, rescue operations, floods, and all kinds of emergencies."

"It is certainly versatile," agreed Kelly.

"Yes, sir. After the eighteen-month Sky Knight evaluation, Los Angeles County Sheriff Peter Pitchess stated that 'The patrol helicopter offers law enforcement its first major breakthrough in crime control since the advent of the radio-equipped patrol car.'"

When the chief crawled out of the helicopter back on the grassy knoll a few minutes later, Ellingsworth asked, "Well chief, what do you think?"

Kelly looked at him and said, "I can see why it is an effective new tool for law enforcement, Bill. One flight convinced me of that."

Wow! It was hard for me to keep from shouting. I'd had some unique situations in my sales experiences, but never had I jumped from chopped liver to prime filet in one flight!

"I suspect there's only one problem," said Kelly, glancing from Ellingsworth over to me, where I stood there beside the helicopter. "It does cost money, does it not, Mr. Kirkland?"

I looked at Kelly, and he was smiling. I smiled back. "Yes, sir. It does. But I think you're gonna be surprised there, too."

He nodded. "I hope you're right, because I am interested. Very interested. But as we say here in Missouri: you're gonna have to show me the numbers."

"I'm prepared to make a financial presentation whenever you're ready, sir."

"How about tomorrow morning at nine o'clock in my office?"

"We'll be there, sir."

He shook hands with all of us, then looked at the helicopter for a moment. "Amazing," he muttered, crawled into the cruiser, and departed.

We all went back to the bar and celebrated. The 269 sat on the grassy knoll beside the Hereford Cow all night, because we weren't in any condition to fly it out.

The next morning, I was surprised to see that Chief Kelly had invited his bureau chiefs and other members of his staff to hear the presentation. I was pleased, of course, but I could sense resistance from the look on their faces.

"This isn't gonna be easy," I whispered to Don as we set up our presentation materials.

"I'm afraid you're right," he whispered back.

"Well, at least we're getting our shot."

The chief looked at me from behind his desk and nodded.

"You may begin when you're ready, Mr. Kirkland."

I made my presentation from charts, explaining the features of the helicopter that made it effective as an airborne patrol car, which was basically what I had covered with Chief Kelly on our demo flight. Then I summarized the objectives of Sky Knight patrol as being able to:

Improve day and night surveillance (to see more).
Improve crime deterrence (to be seen more).
Improve response time.
Increase officer security.
Save resources and money.

I could see the skepticism in the eyes of his staff, but they didn't voice it because they apparently recognized that the chief was interested in the concept.

"Now, gentlemen, let's discuss application effectiveness and cost," I said.

All eyes focused.

"The Sky Knight project proved conclusively that one patrol helicopter can cover thirty-five square miles more effectively, to see and be seen as a deterrent to crime, than a ground patrol car can cover one square mile in the same period of time. It was also able to respond five times faster than the ground unit, on average."

Grumbling and shuffling feet. "I don't believe it," said someone.

"In the eighteen-month Sky Knight project, the city of Lakewood recorded an 8.8 percent *reduction* of part-one crimes [criminal homicide, rape, robbery, assault, burglary, theft, and car theft]. During that same period in Los Angeles County, part-one crime *increased* by 9 percent," I said confidently.

Silence a moment.

"And the cost?" asked the chief.

"Applying the same cost factors to each patrol system, and using current nationally published figures, it will cost you $298.55 for the helicopter as opposed to $1,900.55 for the ground patrol car, to cover the same thirty-five square miles of city streets.

"I don't believe that, either," muttered someone else.

"I'd like to see those figures," said Kelly.

"I have a package of all this data for you, chief," I replied.

"Can I ask a question?" said one of the captains.

"Yes, sir."

"What are you gonna do when you respond to a robbery and the bad guy is down in the street and you're up in the sky?"

"The two big advantages of the airborne patrol car is its superior observation capability, and ability to move quickly in any direction. Once the helicopter is on scene, there is no escape for the suspect. Wherever he goes is reported to the ground units by radio. Bear in mind gentlemen, the helicopter and the ground patrol car work as a team, hand in hand. And the 'eye in the sky' provides a degree of officer security never before enjoyed."

That seemed to register, and I could see some heads nodding, including the chief's.

After Bachali and I had answered all the staff's questions, and they had left the chief's office, Kelly said, "Well, I don't think they are all sold on the idea, but you got their attention . . . and mine. So I'm going to set up a presentation with the city council. If you can convince them, we'll get down to hard cases."

"You got it, chief!" I replied, bubbling with confidence.

I have subsequently made hundreds of presentations to city, county, and state governments across the United States, but I'll never forget that first one to the city council in Kansas City, Missouri. They chewed me up and spit me out in little pieces. And it took all the wind out of my sails.

"Sorry about that, Mr. Kirkland," said the chief as we gathered back in his office after the slaughter. "But I wanted you to see what I'm up against."

I nodded, the words of one councilman still ringing in my ears: "We need a *heeleocopter* like we need a hole in the head!" he'd shrieked. "There is only one way to fight crime. Cops in the street! Cops in the street! And we don't even have the money to do that!"

"Cup of coffee?" asked the chief as he poured himself one.

"I'd rather have as stiff drink," I muttered.

"Me too," he said, grinning. Then he took a sip of coffee and turned thoughtful. "Would it be possible for you fellows to stay here for a couple weeks or so and actually fly on patrol over Kansas City?"

I sat up in my chair. Don looked at me curiously.

"That would be a way of getting some 'show me' data for proof that Sky Knight will reduce crime in Kansas City," said Chief Kelly.

"Why not?" I said, feeling a little breeze slipping back into my sails.

"Richard, I'm going out on a limb with the city council on this thing (this was the first time he called me by my first name). Because I believe that the helicopter, as an adjunct to the ground patrol car, will, indeed, provide a team that can be far more effective in reducing crime than our present system."

"Yes, sir, I'm sure you're right," I agreed.

I called Bill Wyatt later that day, and told him what I wanted to do. Without hesitation, he said go for it. So Bachali and I set up shop at one of the Kansas City Police substations to do around-the-clock helicopter patrol over the city. The chief asked for volunteers from his patrol section to act as flight observers and was swamped with applications.

Since we were going to do twenty-four-hour, day-night patrol, I needed additional pilots, so I hired two experienced helicopter pilots, Bill Evans and Tom Pritchett, from a local helicopter operator, Jerry Getz at Comet Aviation. Then Don and I gave them a quick course in the techniques of airborne police patrol.

"I've checked on it, and there is only one way we can do this legally—that's if you fellows are sworn Kansas City police officers," Kelly said, one morning a few days before we were to begin the program. "And I assume none of you fellows are escaped felons?" he said with a smile.

We shook our heads, then held up our hand and took the oath. We felt pretty cool when we put the shiny Kansas City police officer shield in our coat pocket and strapped on a regulation .38 revolver. I still brag to my grandkids that I was once a gun-toting Kansas City police officer.

Bachali and I held some classes for the six officers who were to be our observers, then did some practice flying. Officers Jim Lohmeyer, William Moulder, Billy Reed, Bill Bumpus, Steve Niebur, and Willaim Dycus were all experienced officers who knew the city and were streetwise, so they adapted quickly. Chief Kelly then made a public announcement of his decision to have a trial Sky Knight program in Kansas City, and Ellingsworth got his editor to give it front-page coverage. I guess some of the city council members were upset, but Kelly held his ground and a few days later we began the program.

We each flew periodic patrols during eight-hour shifts over all sections of the city. But we concentrated on areas of high incidence of part-one crimes, particularly during the hours from about 11 P.M. to 3 A.M.

It was exciting and satisfying and certainly one of my great experiences as a helicopter pilot. The four of us, and our dedicated observers, caught, or were instrumental in catching, a bunch of bad guys, and the stats at the conclusion of

Kansas City Police Chief Clarence Kelly, later director of the FBI, and Captain Jack Brady, commander of the helicopter unit, fall 1968.

our demonstration period proved, without question, that Sky Knight worked over Kansas City equally as well as it had in Lakewood, California.

There were numerous exciting incidents, but I'll just repeat one as an example. As I recall, my observer on this shift was Jim Lohmeyer, but it doesn't matter because they were all great. We were on patrol and got a call from the dispatcher of a bank robbery on the other side of the city. I pulled in full power, and we streaked across town.

When we got there, the robber had left the scene. We did get a description of the getaway car and which way he'd gone, but were unable to find him. So I flew back to the bank and began an expanding-circle search of the area, flying at five hundred feet, scouring the streets, parking lots, and back alleys. As I completed each circle, I expanded out a few blocks, then made another circle.

After about an hour, while flying over an apartment complex, my observer spotted a car that met the description parked under a tree. We circled around and called in the ground units. Within a few minutes they surrounded the area, and not long after that the suspect was apprehended. We had caught ourselves a bank robber.

Armed with the resulting data from our on-scene demonstration, Chief Kelly was able to convince the city fathers that the Sky Knight program would reduce crime in Kansas City, while actually saving them money. Approval was eventually given for the acquisition of three Sky Knight helicopters, and a contract signed with World Associates to train six Kansas City police officers as helicopter pilots. World Associates was established by Captain McDonald to specialize in airborne law enforcement training.

The world's first twenty-four-hour helicopter patrol of a major city began in Kansas City and is still in operation to this day.

Don Bachali and I worked together to establish many other law enforcement helicopter programs through the years in cities across the United States and Canada. But it was particularly satisfying to have been a part of that first major program in Kansas City. Clarence Kelly received national attention for his vision in recognizing the future of helicopters in law enforcement and was subsequently appointed director of the Federal Bureau of Investigation (FBI), replacing J. Edgar Hoover. Years later, Don Bachali and I visited the chief and Bill Ellingsworth, whom Kelly had talked into becoming his public relations officer at FBI headquarters in Washington, D.C., and Kelly said, "See what you fellows and that helicopter got me into?"

6

In the Nam Trenches

After we had visited awhile at our lunch table in the Rosslyn Metro Center in Northern Virginia, I knew that John Harris was the one to tell me a Vietnam story. Men who have gone to war and fought in the trenches have a certain distinctive way of talking about it. If you've been there, you know. And I'd been there many times in a two-seat Sikorsky H-5 helicopter over the rice paddies of Korea. John Harris's trench was a twenty-seven-seat Boeing CH-46 over the jungles of Vietnam.

When I began the search for helicopter tales about Vietnam, I was referred to John by a mutual friend, Darryl Riersgard, who was also a decorated Nam helicopter pilot. He modestly suggested that Harris, who is a Marine program director for Boeing in nearby Washington, D.C., had some hair-raising Nam experiences if I could get him to talk about it.

"I have avoided telling war stories for over thirty years. When I heard others drone on about their experiences, I found it boring and self-serving, so I made a conscious decision to move on, not dwell on the past. But as a favor to Darryl, and because you're one of us, I'll open up the ole memory bank and see what comes out," Harris said to me across our lunch table.

John told me some great stories, enough to make a wonderful book, which made it difficult to choose. But I selected one that I felt would provide some gutsy insight into the reality of what the Marine helicopter crews experienced on a day-to-day basis in Vietnam.

It was hot and sticky without a breath of air coming through the open windows of the hooch [a small, Vietnamese-style house]. Lt. John Harris lay on his cot dressed in a flight suit with his hands folded behind his head, staring into the blackness and wondering what time it was. He knew the other pilots were also restless as he could hear occasional movements in the darkness. He glanced at the luminous dial on his wristwatch. It was almost midnight.

It would be a miserable, tough mission if they had to go. Outside, there was a muggy overcast with low, scuddy clouds, and the night was as black as the inside of a coal-digger's lunchbox. He and his two helo crews were taking their turn pulling standby night medevac, the most harrowing and dangerous of all helicopter missions in Vietnam. Because of the high-risk factor, night missions were limited to operationally essential or emergencies only. However, more often than not, they would be called out.

The flare of a cigarette lighter reflected off the wall. Harris knew it was Joe Martin, his copilot. Martin was a chain-smoker, even at night between periods of sleep. Joe also drank a lot of scotch every night—and he probably wanted a shot now, desperately. But he wouldn't . . . not tonight. Not while on medevac standby. Night missions required skill, concentration, and teamwork from every crew member just to survive.

After awhile, Harris glanced at his watch again. It was almost 0100 hours. Maybe . . . just maybe, they would make it through the night without a call. God, he hoped so.

God wasn't listening this night, and when the field phone rang a few seconds later, it was like a mortar hitting the hooch. All four pilots were off their cots like a shot. Harris grabbed the field phone. After a silent, frozen moment, listening to the crackling voice from the group-operations bunker, he glanced at the probing eyes and said, "Briefing in five, let's go."

Mumbling a few choice superlatives, the Marines grabbed their Kevlar "bullet bouncer" vests and their .38 pistol belts, and hurried out of the hooch into the sultry night. "I'll wake the crew," said Glen "Smokey" Burgess, the pilot of Medevac Two, the backup helicopter. Although alert quarters were available for the enlisted crew, out of pride, they chose to stay with their bird, sleeping on the canvas seats inside the big CH-46.

A few minutes later, the two helicopter medevac crews stood in the pale light of a portable generator, smoking and fidgeting as a briefing officer told them that a team of Marine infantry "grunts" on night patrol in the jungle had engaged the Vietcong in a firefight and had taken serious casualties. They were now trapped by a superior Vietcong force that was moving in for the kill.

Lieutenant Harris, commander of the two-ship medevac team, and every one of his crew knew they had drawn a tough, ugly mission. To attempt a medevac in the jungle under enemy fire was high risk anytime. On a black night in lousy weather, it would be something more like suicide. But Harris and his crew also knew that if they failed to perform their mission, fellow Marines would die on this miserable Vietnam night.

Medevac missions were flown with two helos, as the Marines called them. One helo was lead, designated "Medevac One," and a backup, "Medevac Two." If the lead ship was shot down, the backup would rescue the downed crew, or go down in the attempt. But if success was possible on such a mission, it would be with this workhorse helicopter, the Boeing Vertol CH-46, affectionately nicknamed the "Frog" by its crews. But its ungainly appearance belied its exceptional ability to perform and take brutal punishment.

The CH-46 is a tandem-rotor helicopter with three 50-foot-diameter rotor blades at each end of its fuselage. With a gross weight of over 20,000 pounds, it can carry a crew and twenty-four combat-ready Marines. On this mission, the crew consisted of a pilot, copilot, crew chief, two .50 caliber gunners, and a Navy corpsman, who administered medical aid when required, which was often.

"Okay, guys, let's get them in the air," said Lieutenant Harris as he scribbled on a clip pad the geographical coordinates of the trapped Marines, their radio frequencies, and the frequencies of his top cover—two AH-1 Cobra helicopter gunships.

"Good luck," said the briefing officer.

"Yeah. We'll need it," Harris mumbled, hurrying toward the two darkened shapes on the helipads, where his crew was already scurrying to their assigned positions.

To expedite takeoff, helicopters on standby medevac were given a preflight inspection ahead of time and all checklist items were accomplished down to "engine start." The copilot, Lt. Joe Martin, had already begun that final procedure as Harris pulled himself through the narrow entrance into the cockpit. At a signal from the crew chief that rotor blade tie downs were removed and the area cleared, Harris flipped the start switch and the whine of a General Electric T-58 turbine engine cut the soggy, nightime silence. A few minutes later, the two Marine CH-46 Frogs lifted off the helipad in tandem and flew away into the blackness.

It was like taking off into an inkwell, and within seconds the helicopter was engulfed in the misting overcast. Harris knew that he had no choice but to fly on instruments until he could get above the clouds where, hopefully, starlight would provide some visibility. After a quick radio transmission to advise the backup pilot of his intentions, he pulled collective to climb power and started up.

The cloud layer was filled with muggy air and the helicopter pitched and yawed as it climbed, causing the instruments to bounce erratically. But after a relatively short flight, they broke out on top of the cloud layer and into a dark but clear sky.

"Thanks for little favors," Harris muttered to himself, then quickly pressed the transmit switch: "You with me, Medevac Two?"

"I'm right off your starboard, Medevac One," replied Lieutenant Burgess, pilot of the backup helicopter.

Harris glanced over his right shoulder through the side cockpit window and saw the glow of the backup helo's clearance lights. "Okay, Glen. I make it a heading of 320 degrees for about twenty-five minutes. When we get there, we'll assess conditions and go from there."

"Roger."

Switching to intercom, Harris said, "Take it, Joe, while I recheck these coordinates."

"I got it," replied the copilot, taking the flight controls.

Snapping on a penlight, Harris rechecked his chart. He was confident he could find the coordinate location by using the azimuth and distance off the Danang TACAN [radio aid]. But then how in the world was he going to find the exact spot where the Marines were trapped if it was covered by an overcast? All he could hope for was a break in the clouds.

As they approached the area, Harris called his cover, the two AH-1 Cobra gunships.

"Roger, Medevac One. We're circling the area now, but it's socked in so we can't pinpoint the target," one of the Cobra pilots replied.

"Jesus, now what'a we gonna do?" groaned Martin.

"Firefly, this is Medevac One, do you read?" transmitted Harris, as he put the CH-46 into a wide circle over the area where the trapped Marines, codenamed Firefly, were supposed to be.

No answer.

Harris repeated his radio call.

After the third call: "They are either already wiped out or we're in the wrong place," said Martin.

"Lieutenant Harris, I heard something that time. It was real faint but I heard it," said the crew chief over the intercom.

"Firefly, if you're down there speak up!" barked Harris.

This time a reply came, but in a barely discernible whisper: "We're here. . . . We're here, Med One. . . . But I can't talk loud because Charlie's so close we can hear them talking."

"Oh great," said someone.

"Can you hear the helicopters, Firefly?" asked Harris.

"Yeah. We can hear you up there."

"Okay, Firefly. You got any ceiling down there?"

The next transmission was too weak to hear.

"Can't hear you, Firefly."

"Gotta speak low . . . Charlie's real close. . . . It's pitch black down here . . . can't see anything. Can you make it? They're closing in on us."

"Stand by, Firefly." Harris switched to intercom and spoke to his crew: "This is a real shit sandwich, guys. Our only chance to save those grunts is to try and find a break in the overcast, then drop down under it, and have them talk us into their LZ [landing zone] by sound. We'll be down there alone with no Cobra cover, so we'll take ground fire. It's a long shot but as I see it, the only shot."

"We're ready, sir," replied the chief.

Yeah, they were ready, said John Harris to himself. Not that they had a choice. As the aircraft commander, he made the decision. They went wherever he took them. But John knew those brave men back there at their crew stations would fly that helo to hell with him. Their pride and dedication never ceased to amaze him.

Switching back to transmit, Harris briefed the ground-based Direct Air Support Controller, Medevac Two, and the Cobra gunships of his intentions.

"There may not be any ceiling under the clouds, Medevac One," advised one of the gunships.

Harris knew what the gunship pilot was saying: if there was no ceiling under the clouds, he wouldn't be able to see the trees in the darkness and would probably fly the helicopter straight into the jungle. "Yeah, I know," he muttered on the radio.

"Medevac One, this is Two. You want me to follow you down?"

Harris glanced out at the flashing red anticollision light on the backup helo that was just off his starboard side. "No. You stay above the overcast and orbit with the Cobras. If we don't make it, it'll be your call, Glen."

"Roger."

"Medevac One from Cobra lead. I think I saw a small break in the clouds just this side of that ridge at your nine o'clock position."

"Thanks, we'll check it out," said Harris as he banked the CH-46 toward the dark ridgeline that jutted up from the gray overcast on his port side.

Radio silence for a few minutes.

"There's a hole in the overcast over here all right, and we're gonna go for it. Firefly, do you read?"

"I read you," came the whispered transmission.

"Okay. We're coming down lights out, and if we make it you gotta direct us to you by sound, using clock positions. You got it?"

"Got it."

"All right, good guys," said Harris to his crew. "When the bad guys hear us coming, they're gonna throw the kitchen sink at us. So everybody got your bullet bouncers on?"

The crew all responded in the affirmative, and both pilots rotated their .38 caliber pistol holsters around from their hip so that they covered the family jewels—a habit most Vietnam helicopter pilots practiced.

In the CH-46 the pilots sat in armor-plated seats with "wings" on each side, so they were protected from small-arms fire from the rear, bottom, and each side. The kevlar "bullet bouncers" protected chest and stomach, which left jewels, arms, legs, and head exposed. The other crew members wore the Kevlar vests but without armor plate; they were significantly more exposed. They accepted this risk as part of their duty.

"It's gonna be black down there, so everybody keep a sharp eye out, and if you see something, sound off. Gunners, don't fire unless I give the order, I don't want to give Charlie a target," instructed Harris.

"Yeah, they can't see us any more than we can see them," added the copilot, switching off all outside navigation lights.

Harris punched his UHF transmit switch. "Das control, this is Medevac One. We're goin' in."

"Roger, Medevac One, we copy," replied the air controller.

"Okay, here we go," said Harris, pushing the cyclic forward and easing off the collective, which nosed the helicopter into the black hole in the overcast. It was sure enough the black hole of destiny, thought Harris, straining to see something ahead . . . something to get spatial orientation. If he got vertigo all would be lost. Nothing but blackness . . . swirling blackness. . . .

"Trees dead ahead!" snapped the copilot.

Harris saw the dark shapes loom over the nose and pulled collective as he hauled back on the cyclic. The big bird shuttered and pitched up, skimming over the treetops with only inches to spare.

After a moment to let his pounding heart slow, Harris came on the intercom. "Okay. We're here, everyone on your toes and—"

"Medevac One from Firefly, we hear you."

"Give me direction, Firefly."

"I think you're to the north of us."

"Give it to me by clock positions."

"There is a ridge just off our starboard, lieutenant," advised the crew chief.

Harris glanced out and saw the dim outline in the darkness. "Got it, chief."

"Medevac One, this is Two. How you doin' down there?"

"We're doin', Two. We're below the overcast. Stand by. Firefly, give me a clock number."

"You're goin' away from us."

"Okay, I'm making a one-eighty," replied Harris, rolling the CH-46 into a bank. Now flying lights out, he must maintain spatial orientation by visual reference to the black shapes below him. This was tricky and demanding flying, and one mistake would plunge the helicopter into the jungle in a deadly crash.

"I can hear you coming back toward us."

"Good, you got the LZ marked?"

"Arely . . . too . . . oss . . . ant . . . ow . . . airs . . ."

"Can't read you, Firefly."

Silence.

"Charlie's too close. Can't use flares," came the weak reply from the trapped Marine.

"Damn, John. There ain't no way you can land in that friggin' inkwell without some kind of marker," rasped Martin over the intercom.

John knew that his copilot was correct. He would be fortunate just to keep the bird flying under these conditions. Trying to land could only result in the loss of the helicopter and six more Marines in addition to those below whose fate, at best, hung in the balance.

"You're going off to the east. . . . Uh, come right, we're at your . . . I think, three o'clock position."

"Correcting right."

Silence.

Lt. John Harris beside his Boeing CH-46 helicopter, Vietnam, summer 1969. (Courtesy Lt. John Harris)

"Ooo . . . com . . . ight . . . ard . . . uz."

"Repeat your last transmission."

"You're comin' right toward us."

"Okay. But I got to have some kind of reference to land with, Firefly. You have to mark the LZ somehow."

"Ground fire coming up, lieutenant!" shouted the crew chief. Suddenly the blackness was pierced with lines of glowing fireballs. The Vietcong were firing at the sound of the helicopter, and their tracers were spewing in all directions.

"Gunners, hold your fire!" snapped Harris over the intercom. He could see the Vietcong fire was inaccurate, but if he returned fire his tracers would give them a target. He would hold off firing as long as possible.

"You flew directly over us!" shouted Firefly.

Harris put the helo into a right bank, and, glancing back, he could see the arches of enemy ground fire coming up from the area he'd just passed over. Now he had a bracket on where the grunts were trapped. But it would do him no good, because it was just as pitch black as everything else.

"Firefly, there is no way I can get to you unless you mark an LZ."

Silence.

"Medevac One, how about if I hold up my cigarette lighter?"

"A cigarette lighter?" said Martin.

"When I hear you getting close I'll hold it up so you can see it, okay?" In a sort of pleading voice.

"I don't think that's gonna work, Firefly."

Silence for a moment. "Medevac One . . . we're in serious trouble down here. We got wounded, and Charlie's moving in fast. We're goners if you can't get us soon."

"Firefly, you sure that's all you can mark the LZ with is a cigarette lighter?"

"We're surrounded by Vietcong on three sides, but there is a clear area between some trees on the one side. I can hold the lighter so it can only be seen from that direction."

A moment of silence.

John Harris took a deep breath. He was faced with an agonizing dilemma. He had his own crew of good men to consider, and to land the CH-46 in the jungle, on a black night, under fire, with nothing to guide him but a cigarette lighter, was madness. But to fly away, condemning those other good men to death, was something he couldn't bring himself to do. He punched the intercom and said to his crew: "You all heard the story. As fellow Marines, we owe it those grunts to give it a shot."

"We're ready back here, sir," came the expected reply from the crew chief, and similar comments followed from the other crew members.

"Okay. Stand by for an LZ landing. Hold your fire till I give the command."

"John, this is Glen. Whatta you gonna do?"

"We're goin' in, Glen. Stand by."

"The ground fire stopped, lieutenant," said the crew chief over the intercom.

"Yeah. I see it did. Firefly, give me a reading."

"You went off to the south of us. . . . Uh, turn left, I'd guess about your three o'clock position."

Another silence.

"Okay. . . . Sounds like you're headed back toward us."

Maintaining orientation was precarious for the Marine pilot. His only reference was the dim horizon created by the slight difference in darkness between the ground plane and the cloud layer. Now he must make an approach and land in a sea of blackness guided by a cigarette lighter. He was reminded that Navy pilots claim landing on an aircraft carrier at night is the most demanding of all. He'd take that in a New York second over what he was about to attempt.

"You're getting close. Medevac One. Come left a little."

Harris kicked pedal slightly and eased down on the collective and back on the cyclic control, slowing the helicopter's forward speed.

"You're close . . . close," came the whispered advisory.

"I can see trees, lieutenant. We're about a hundred feet," reported the crew chief hanging out of the crew door.

"Okay, Firefly, light up," instructed Harris.

"My Zippo's on. Can you see it?"

The two marine pilots stared through the CH-46 windshield.

"I see it dead ahead!" barked Martin.

Focusing on the tiny, flickering light in the black world ahead, Harris eased the helicopter forward in a slow gradual decent. "Sound off if you see obstacles!" he instructed the crew.

"Ground fire!" snapped the chief as the darkness exploded in streams of burning fireballs all around the helicopter.

"Stay on the instruments, Joe!" Harris instructed his copilot, knowing that, in this type of blackout flying under fire, engine and rotor RPM and torque could vary dangerously.

Harris felt perspiration run into his eyes as the helicopter shuttered out of translational lift and began its transition to ground effect. "About thirty feet, lieutenant. Steady as you go," he heard the crew chief say from his precarious perch at the crew door.

"You're over the LZ!" shouted Firefly as the wind from the big fifty-foot rotor blades swept down over the trapped Marines, blowing out the cigarette lighter.

"Move left! Left! We're over a tree!" shouted the crew chief.

Harris felt his heart leap as the controls jerked violently in his hands. He knew the rotor blades had struck something . . . probably a tree. But he'd done that before and knew those big blades could take a beating. Of course, there was a limit to that beating, and when reached, the bird would thrash itself to pieces in a matter of seconds.

"Okay, okay! You're clear, lieutenant. You can set her down," said the chief.

As Harris fought to bring the ten-ton helicopter to a blackout landing, Martin hit the back-ramp switch. "Ramp going down!" he shouted.

"We're taking hits!" reported one of the gunners.

"Get 'em aboard quick!" commanded Harris.

The grunts, carrying their wounded, scrambled up the ramp and into the helo the second it slammed down, its big rotor blades slicing the jungle growth like giant machetes.

Harris's heart pounded and perspiration stung his eyes as he grasped the controls, maintaining full rotor RPM, ready to pull in everything the engines would give him the instant the crew chief cleared him to go. He cringed from the distinctive hollow sound of lead piercing aluminum. But he knew the helicopter would take a lot of hits and still fly away. The engines and hydraulic lines were protected by armor plating. The rotor, however, was not. A critical hit there and . . .

"All aboard! Go! Go!," shouted the crew chief.

Harris pulled in all the power he could get, and the Frog leaped out of the LZ, its rotor blades slicing and spewing pieces of tree limbs and foliage in all directions as it cut a swath out of the jungle.

"Okay gunners, give 'em a taste of their own medicine!" instructed Harris, and a second later the two .50-caliber guns roared from the cabin of the CH-46, sending a deadly fusillade into the jungle below.

"How you doing down there, Medevac One?" came the voice of Glen Burgess, from the backup helicopter.

"Clear the area, Smokey! We're coming upstairs like a homesick angel!" replied Harris.

"You got the grunts?"

"We got 'em."

"Great job, Medevac One," transmitted one of the Cobra gunships, circling above the overcast.

The CH-46 Marine helicopter popped up through the overcast a few minutes later, and Harris leveled the big bird out, flipped on his navigation and anticollision lights, and headed for the nearest field hospital.

"How do the controls feel, John?" asked Martin, concerned over the heavy vibrations in the helicopter.

"She's a little rough on the controls. We probably knocked off a few chunks of blade chopping trees, but she'll get us home."

"Okay. You want me to relieve you for a bit?"

"Yeah, you got the controls."

"I got 'er," said Martin.

"Medevac One, this is control. Understand you made the pickup?"

"That's a roger, control."

"Good show, Medevac One."

As always, after a mission that brought death so close, the intercom in the Marine helo suddenly became quiet for a few moments while each crew member did his own thing: a silent prayer or just his own private thoughts.

Then, over the intercom, "Lieutenant Harris?"

"Yeah?"

"Uh, this is the chief, sir. You mind if I tell you something?"

"Fire away, chief."

"I just wanted to say, sir, you've really got your shit together."

John Harris looked across the lunch table at me, there in the Rosslyn Metro Center restaurant. "Ya know, I've thought about it a lot all these years, and I'm still in awe of the unwavering dedication, bravery, and skill of those helicopter crewmen in Vietnam. Day after day in miserable conditions, the maintenance crews kept those choppers flying, and the crew chiefs, gunners, and the corpsmen would crawl in and do their duty on those high-risk missions. Many of them were killed. I didn't know then, and I still don't know, what motivated them. But I do know one thing: they were genuine American heros."

Harris glanced out the window for a moment, then added: "They awarded me a Distinguished Flying Cross for that mission, and I'm proud of it, even though I've long forgotten the words on the citation. But I'll tell you something, Richard." He hesitated and grinned. "I will never forget those simple words from my crew chief that night. That was the most precious compliment I've ever received and one I'll remember the rest of my life."

9

Cayuse

I was in Las Vegas in the fall of 1970 on a sales trip and somehow got invited to dinner with my big boss, Ray Hopper. He was vice president and general manager of Hughes Tool Company, Aircraft Division. That made him the head man in our company because there was only one president in the Hughes empire: Howard Hughes. That evening the two of us met at the Desert Inn bar for a before-dinner cocktail. I was a bit nervous, naturally, because I was just a helicopter salesman and only on rare occasions fraternized with the company executives.

While we were visiting, it suddenly dawned on me that Ray Hopper was a long-time associate and confidant of Howard Hughes, who, at that very moment, was upstairs in the penthouse. Dare I ask Hopper any questions about Hughes?

After our second drink, Hopper seemed to be in a talkative mood, and I got up enough courage to ask: "Mr. Hopper, is Mr. Hughes pleased with the success of the Cayuse?"

The Cayuse was an observation-class helicopter built by Hughes for the Army in the 1960s. It had an articulated, four-bladed, twenty-six-foot rotor system, powered by an Allison C-18 turbine engine. It could carry a pilot and three passengers, and was used primarily as an air-cavalry scout in the Vietnam War.

Hopper hesitated, and I couldn't tell whether he was thinking about my question or if he just thought it was presumptuous of me to ask. He was a handsome, husky man with dark hair and penetrating eyes. Finally he nodded. "Yeah, he's pleased all right, but all I hear is a lot of squalling about how much it cost him."

I was in the commercial sales division of the company, so all I knew about the 06A Cayuse, winning the Army's light-observation helicopter (LOH) contract, was secondhand information. Anybody who knew the real story didn't talk about it because of Howard's fetish for secrecy. Well, Hopper was somebody who knew the real story, but did I dare ask him about it?

I did. And for the next hour or so, I enjoyed a fascinating and enlightening conversation, which went something like this:

"Howard always wanted to get a Hughes airframe into the military inventory, you know," offered Hopper.

"He did?" I responded quickly, sitting on the edge of my chair.

"Yeah. He's gotten a number of research and development contracts where we just built one or two items, but never a full-production contract, and he'd been trying for years to get one. Then, ironically, when he finally does get an Army contract, it's for a helicopter."

I was taken aback by Hopper's comment. "Uh, you mean he doesn't like helicopters?"

Hopper took a sip of his drink. "I wouldn't say he dislikes them. It's just that he couldn't be a hands-on participant in the Cayuse program like he had in his past aviation projects. He has always been personally involved with the design of his airplanes and is one of the sharpest aeronautical engineers I have ever seen, even though he doesn't have an engineering degree. He is also one hell of a pilot, having personally set all kinds of world records in aircraft he designed and built. But as far as I know, he's never set foot in a helicopter."

"Never flown a helicopter?" I croaked incredulously. It was hard to believe that an aviator like Howard Hughes would not have flown his own helicopter.

"No . . . he hasn't."

"That's a shame, because any pilot who enjoys flying as Mr. Hughes obviously does would love a high-performing helicopter like the Cayuse."

Hopper nodded. "Yeah. He probably would. Howard always loves a challenge. And the tougher it is, the better he likes it."

"Well, learning to fly a helicopter is a bit of a challenge, all right. But I'm sure it wouldn't take Mr. Hughes long to master it." Suddenly I had a great idea. Chock it up to naiveté or two martinis: "Uh . . . I'm a helicopter instructor. I'd be pleased to teach him?"

Hopper smiled.

I took another gulp of my martini and added, "Perhaps you could mention it when you see him?"

Hopper looked at me and laughed. "I haven't seen Howard Hughes in years."

I looked at him in astonishment.

He took a sip of his drink. "All my dealings with Howard nowadays are with little handwritten notes or over the telephone."

"But . . . isn't he . . . just upstairs?" I asked, pointing a finger upward.

"Yeah, but he doesn't allow anyone but his aides up there anymore, and I don't think he's been out of that penthouse since he bought this hotel in 1967. He's completely isolated himself."

I knew that he was rarely seen out in public these days, but the scuttlebutt around the company was that he'd just gotten more secretive and actually came out of the penthouse at night incognito. One of the guys who worked at our production facility in Culver City told me that a night guard said that Hughes often flew into the plant late at night and worked with the engineers on the Cayuse design. I'd also heard that he regularly went to see his wife, movie star Jean Peters, in Bel Air.

But here was Ray Hopper, the one person who would know, telling me that what I'd heard was nothing but rumors and that in truth he was now a recluse. This was hard to believe, because Hughes had been such a dynamic legend in the industrial, motion-picture, and aviation world.

I don't know if Hopper felt a need to explain, or if he was just in a rare mood to talk about a forbidden subject. Whatever the motivation, he said, "Yes, he's a recluse now, but let me tell you, Richard, he was a dynamo and, in a strange way, still is. You know he was the driving force in the design of the H-1 racer, in which he personally broke the world speed record in 1935. And it was the same when we were building the flying boat. It was his drive and vision that kept that project going until it was completed. The H-1 flying boat was the largest aircraft ever flown, and he flew it.

"He personally did the test flying on all his aircraft, and, when he was testing the XH-11, the world's fastest reconnaissance aircraft at that time, he stayed with it on its death plunge, trying to figure out what the problem was. It crashed and exploded, and Howard got burns on sixty-five percent of his body. And he'd already been in two other crashes that damn-near killed him.

"He's a battered man, all right, but still amazing and involved in a whole bunch of things that he conducts primarily over the telephone," said Hopper, taking another sip of his drink.

I said, "I know he's done some great things in the aviation world. Did he get intimately involved in the Cayuse program?"

"Like I said, he wasn't into the nuts and bolts as he had been on earlier projects. But he was involved, and his engineers designed and fabricated the 06A utilizing a bunch of his ideas, which involved advanced technology and a 'simplicity of design' concept. And the finished product, the Cayuse, exceeded even our expectations. As you know, we set twenty-three world-helicopter-performance records in the Cayuse. That's more than any airframe in history in its class."

"Wasn't its performance the reason Hughes won the LOH contract?"

Hopper chuckled and said, "Yes. But there was a lot more to it than just the performance. You see, this whole program dates back to the mid-1950s. At the end of the Korean War the Army knew it was gonna get into the helicopter business, big time. One of their initial requirements was for a light-observation helicopter, which, at that time, they envisioned as a two-man, piston powered, 'Flying Jeep.' That prompted us to design and build the little 269 helicopter to meet that requirement.

"Then later, the Army changed its mind, deciding they wanted a turbine-powered, four-place LOH. That necessitated a change in the request for proposal, so it was back to the drawing board. But the procurement gurus in Washington didn't believe we were qualified to bid on that requirement. We pointed out that Hughes had already built and flew the world's largest helicopter, the XH-17 flying crane, and the XV-9A, the world's only hot-cycle helicopter ever to fly [hot cycle is where the turbine gases turn the rotor]. That, and some of Howard's arm twisting via telephone, encouraged them to relent and let us submit a bid."

"And then you won the contract?"

"Not yet. We had to prove the performance in a flyoff, then go through the bidding exercise as part of the competitive procurement process. And that's when Howard put his money where his mouth was, to quote an old saying. We knew we had the best helicopter, and it met or exceeded all the performance specifications the Army had set. But now we had to have the lowest price, and that's where Howard stepped up to the plate. He sold the Cayuse to the Army at a price that won the contract, all right. But it also cost Howard Hughes over a hundred million dollars."

"Holly schmolly!" I exclaimed.

"Well, Howard was determined to get a Hughes airframe into the Army inventory and was willing to take the financial hit. Of course, I took the hit over how much it cost him. He's still squawking at me about that. But he's proud of the Cayuse and so is everyone else who had a hand in its development and production," said Hopper.

The Hughes 06A "Cayuse" over a Vietnam battlefield, late 1969.

"I have friends who flew it in Vietnam, and they say it's a great helicopter," I said.

Hopper nodded. "Yeah. The Army proved in Vietnam that the 'Loach' [nickname for Cayuse] is ideal for the light-observation mission, particularly as an air-cavalry scout on the battlefield. Army accident records also substantiate that it ushered in a whole new level of helicopter safety and crash worthiness."

I added, "I read about one Army pilot who was on a scout mission and got two of the four rotor blades shot up so bad that he had to crash land in enemy territory. Before the Vietcong could get to him, he and his observer crawled up on the rotor head, took the two damaged blades off, and then flew the bird out of there on the two remaining rotor blades. He said it shook something awful, but it got him home."

"That was one for the record books," said Hopper.

"Yes, sir. And I think the U.S. Army and the American taxpayer got a real bargain with the Hughes Cayuse," I said.

The Hughes Tool Company, Aircraft Division, produced and delivered nearly 1,400 06A Cayuse helicopters for the Army during the Vietnam War. Howard Hughes's long-time dream of having one of his aircraft serve in the U.S. military was fulfilled, and the Army aviation journals abound with incredible stories of its feats on the battlefield.

10

The Game

This is a personal account of the helicopter combat missions flown by U.S. Army pilot Warrant Officer William Q. Kirk on a spring day in Vietnam in 1968. Other than editing and some dialog translation, this is his story in his words.

Listening to the briefing officer that morning emphasize "shoot anything that moves," I suspected this mission was going to be a rough one—but, then again, most of them were. It was just that some were worse than others, and we T-Birds [our call sign] were playing a rough game. It was called "Kill or Be Killed."

I was the pilot of a Bell UH-1B "Huey" gunship assigned to the 336th Assault Helicopter Company at Soc Trang Army Airfield, South Vietnam. On this particular day, I was the leader of a two-ship fire team that had been assigned to fly low over the LZ [landing zone], where a combat assault operation was to take place. Our job was to reconnaissance the area for any sign of enemy activity and see if we could draw fire. Although that was our normal procedure for this type of mission, I felt that concept was fundamentally flawed. We got shot at enough without asking for it.

The theory was, however, that it was better for us to take fire than the troop-carrier "slicks" [helicopters] that transported the soldiers into the LZ after we'd cleared the way. But the Vietcong wouldn't usually give away their position until the slicks came in because they were juicier targets: they couldn't shoot back, and we could. Sometimes, when their positions were heavily fortified or our gunships were just too inviting a target, we got what we were looking for: big trouble.

After our 0500 mission briefing that morning, my crew and I, designated T-Bird 4, and my wingman, T-Bird 8, trudged to the flightline with our gear and crawled into our birds. Each crew consisted of a pilot, copilot, crew chief, and gunner. The Hueys were armed with fourteen 2.75-inch rockets, seven in each external pod on the side of the helicopter, which I fired, and three thousand rounds of 7.62mm bullets for the machine guns, also mounted on each side, which were operated by the copilot. The crew chief and gunner in the back of the helicopter each had a M60 machine gun with five hundred rounds and a box of grenades. With all that, and a full load of fuel, we were overweight, and it was a struggle to get off the ground, but my wingman and I both managed it and headed off over the jungle. About twenty minutes later we arrived over the AO [area of operation] at 1,000 feet.

I scanned the area and identified the LZ, which was a group of interlaced rice paddies surrounded by jungle. It looked peaceful enough, as all I could see were Vietnamese farmers working their paddies. I called my wingman on the radio and advised that we would descend and do a low-level reconnaissance. I pulled my rocket sight into position in front of me and lowered my bullet-proof helmet visor.

"Okay, we're goin' down. Everybody get your protectors on," I said over the intercom to my crew. We wore chest protectors in the cockpit and had armor-plated seats. The gun crew wore chest and back armor plates.

"Keep a sharp eye out," I added as I pushed the cyclic forward and nosed the Huey down to the treetops, leveled off, and flew low across the paddies. I could see there were a couple hundred Vietnamese that appeared to be women, children, and old men. They all kept their heads down. Not a one looked up at the helicopter as we flew over. I was aware that my orders were to shoot anything that moved in the LZ, but I could see no threat from these farmers, and opening fire on them would be like slaughtering sheep.

"T-Bird 4, this is T-Bird lead, we're not going to fire on those farmers."

"Don't fire on 'em?"

"That's affirmative. Do not fire."

After zigzagging over the LZ for about fifteen minutes, I called my wingman again: "T-Bird 8 from T-Bird 4, what's your take on it?"

"I don't see any indication of Vietcong, T-Bird 4."

"Neither do I, but I got an uncomfortable feeling. Let's make another pass around before I call Delta 6 with a go for troop insertion."

Delta 6 was the Army colonel in command of the combat assault. He operated from the command-and-control [C&C] helicopter that orbited 3,000 feet above the AO. Once I gave him a green light, he would then call in the troop-carrier helicopters that were standing by.

As I made one last pass over the LZ, I somehow sensed the Vietcong were there; and my instincts were correct. We were suddenly flying into a sea of fireballs coming out of the trees along the border of the paddies. I guess the temptation was just too much for the enemy gunners.

"We're taking hits!" shrieked my crew chief on the intercom.

I slammed the bird into a bank and keyed the mic: "T-Bird 8, we're under fire from the treeline, get 'em with your rockets!"

My wingman was behind me and in a better position to take out the gun position with his rockets, but he was also under fire and had to bank away.

"T-Bird 8 is hit, and my gunner is wounded!" he shouted.

"Let's get out of here!" I replied and headed away from the trees where the fire was coming from.

We flew out a ways to some open rice paddies to assess our damage. As it turned out, both helicopters had taken numerous hits, but nothing vital and we were operating normally. The gunner on T-Bird 8 had stopped the bleeding of a shoulder wound and reported that he was all right.

I called Delta 6 and advised the colonel I had wounded aboard and was returning to base, but would take out the Vietcong gun position in the LZ before I departed, because I knew exactly where it was.

Although Delta 6 was in command, the fire-team leader ran the combat assault show, and it was a lot of responsibility. He had to fly the helicopter, read the map, know the enemy locations, understand the friendly locations and their intentions, shoot rockets, and direct the machine-gun fire. He also had to work four radios at the same time: the copilot and crew on intercom, the wingman on VHF, C&C and the transport helicopters on UHF, and the ground troops on FM. He was also responsible for the safety of his crew and the crew of his wingman, reconning and securing the LZ, defining the approach and departure routes for the transport helicopters, providing cover for the slicks during insertions and extractions, evaluating objectives, defining enemy positions and taking them out, and providing cover for the ground troops.

That was a lot of responsibility for a twenty-two-year-old kid, whose world eighteen months earlier had been college parties and girls. I couldn't even have told you where Vietnam was before I got drafted. It's not that I didn't love my country, I just hadn't planned on fighting for it. Well, surprise. Courtesy of my friendly draft board, I was selected to do just that. Preferring flying to walking, I volunteered for helicopter-pilot training and got two months of basic training, nine months of flight school, and an all-expenses-paid trip across the Pacific Ocean.

When I arrived in Saigon and found out what the life expectancy of a combat helicopter pilot was, I immediately volunteered to fly the general. I figured generals didn't get too close to combat. However, much to my dismay, my request was denied, and I was assigned to the transport platoon of the 336th Assault Helicopter Company. After three months of flying troop transports, taking fire and not being able to shoot back, I raised my level of insanity. I volunteered for assignment to the gun platoon. If I was going to take fire, I was going to return fire. Now I wasn't avoiding trouble, I was looking for it. That's what gunship pilots do. It was the game—Kill or Be Killed.

My gunner had thrown out smoke grenades where we'd taken fire, so when we flew back over the LZ the smoke was still visible along the treeline, revealing the Vietcong's position.

"We're goin' in, give it to 'em!" I told my crew on the intercom, then switched to transmit. "Let's take 'em out, T-Bird 8," I said as I started my firing run.

"I'm right behind you, T-Bird 4!" replied my wingman.

The enemy gunners opened fire on us again, but my first two rockets were right on target, and my copilot and cabin gunners shredded the jungle with a fusillade of deadly machine-gun fire. After the third run we had expended our ammunition, but there was no more fire coming our way.

I reported to the colonel at C&C: "Delta 6, this is T-Bird lead, we silenced them, but I suspect there's Vietcong still in there, so mark this area as hot. We're headed for Soc Trang with our wounded and to check battle damage. You'll have to get another fire team to cover the insertion."

"Roger, T-Bird 8. But I need you back here as soon as possible, as we're short on gunships."

"Roger, Delta 6." Then to my wingman: "Okay, T-Bird 8, let's head for the barn."

As we banked away I glanced down at the rice paddies that had been full of Vietnamese farmers a few minutes ago. They were all gone. They had been decoys and could have gotten us all killed. I wondered what I would do the next time I faced women and children with orders to shoot anything that moved.

After landing back at Soc Trang, we found that T-Bird 8 had taken seventeen hits with damage to the flight controls and fuel cells, so it was grounded. My bird had taken twelve hits in the tailboom, in the underside of the fuselage, and in the main rotor blades, but it was still flyable. I told my crew chief that I also sensed bullets penetrating right over my head. He looked but couldn't find any holes. The guys gave me a hard time about exaggerating the situation. About that time, the crew chief, who had climbed on top of the helicopter to look at the main rotor blades again, hollered at me to come up. I climbed up, and he showed me two bullet holes above the pilot's seat, about an inch from my head.

T-Bird 8 was assigned another helicopter, and two hours later both gunships were armed, refueled, and ready to return to the operational area. We got a replacement for the wounded gunner and struggled into the air again.

As soon as we were airborne, I checked in with Delta 6 and he directed me to stand by at a tactical-staging area that had been set up near the LZ. Another gun team from the 121st Assault Helicopter Company, call sign "Viking," was on station working with the ground commanders and had covered the insertion of troop carriers into the LZ without incident.

We landed at the staging area, shut down, and waited for further direction. The staging area was a plot of earth the size of a football field within a large rice paddy. There are no trees in rice paddies. The temperature was now approaching 100 degrees, the humidity was stifling, and the mosquitoes were hungry. The crew chief and gunner took refuge in the back of the helicopter. The only shade my copilot and I could find was under the tailboom, where we were fair game for all the bugs. Being shot at was almost preferable.

Things were going slowly in the AO. The ground troops were encountering no resistance, but that's par for the course. The South Vietnamese troops didn't look for the enemy very hard. They didn't want to fight. What were they fighting for? Their government was corrupt, their military leaders were inept, their training was inadequate, and they were not paid well. Their objective on a military operation was not to make contact with the enemy if they could help it. But I guess they figured that as long as they were there, they would take advantage of the opportunity to steal the farmer's chickens and whatever other meager belongings they could carry off. Not exactly the way to win the hearts and minds of the people. For most Vietnamese the war was cruel.

After our leisurely lunch of tasteless C-rations, we were launched by Delta 6 to assist the ground troops in the LZ. After an hour and a half of searching the

Warrant Officer Bill Kirk (sitting at far right) and his crew beside UH-1, T-Bird 4 gunship at Soc Trang Army Airfield, Vietnam, spring 1968. (Courtesy Bill Kirk)

jungle for bad guys and laying in a couple of rocket and machine-gun strikes on suspected Vietcong positions, we returned to Soc Trang to refuel and rearm.

Operations called about 1600 and advised us to plan on the slicks arriving at the LZ for troop extraction at 1645. Our T-Birds would be the primary fire team, and the Vikings, the other fire team, would remain in the staging area as backup. After receiving an update on the location of the ground troops and the plan for extraction, my wingman and I launched again and proceeded to the AO. There, I got confirmation from Delta 6 on the LZ and troop locations.

My wingman and I then flew a reconnaissance of the LZ and identified approach and departure routes for the slicks. The extraction would be done with fourteen troop-carrying helicopters, each carrying one "stick" of twelve to fourteen troops.

I made radio contact with the slick leader and gave him directions for landing and departure that avoided suspected enemy areas. As the slicks approached the LZ, my wingman and I took up positions on each side of the formation.

When the transport helicopters had settled into the LZ, T-Bird 8 and I then set up a low-level orbit around the rice paddy. All was well until I noticed a flash off the right side of my helicopter. Then the LZ exploded in a barrage of mortar and automatic weapons.

"We're taking fire! We're taking fire!" screamed the slick leader over the UHF radio, as explosions mushroomed everywhere.

I saw a mortar hit in the middle of one of the troop sticks as they waited to board the helicopter. Several Vietnamese soldiers catapulted head over heels into the air as though they were rag dolls. Now the radio was filled with voices screaming about taking fire, including my wingman, T-Bird 8. My own crew chief and gunner shouted on the intercom that we were taking hits.

"Return fire! Return fire!" I ordered, and a second later the bird shook as my copilot and gunners opened up with everything they had.

At that moment, Delta 6, who must have been asleep, called for an update briefing on the extraction progress before even listening to his radio, which pissed me off something awful.

"We're under fire! Mortars in the LZ! Get the fuck off the radio!" I yelled at the colonel.

As I scanned the area for the sources of the enemy fire, I saw a slick take a direct hit and explode, spewing bodies and pieces of helicopter in all directions. A piece of wreckage struck the rotor of the nearest chopper and it began to disintegrate. Now I had two transports down, and as I watched, a Vietnamese soldier ran into the tail rotor of a departing chopper, which decapitated him and caused the pilot to lose control. The Huey lurched into the air spinning violently, then plunged back into the rice paddy and beat itself to death, hurtling broken pieces across the paddy, like shrapnel, mutilating everything in its path.

The transports were now trying to takeoff, with or without troops. But with no gun cover, they were like sitting ducks and taking terrible punishment. The South Vietnamese troops were pinned down in the LZ and offering little resistance. I needed to get them to start firing into the treelines to curb the enemy gunners, but the radio was clogged with screaming voices and I couldn't get through to the ground commanders.

"Delta 6, scramble Viking! Scramble Viking!" I yelled, hoping my transmission would get through as I needed gunship help, and I needed it fast.

"Let's go, T-Bird 8!" I shouted on the radio as I spotted a source of fire. "Follow me in!" I added, banking toward the treeline. We swooped down across the LZ, all guns blazing and both of us firing rockets into the trees where I'd seen muzzle flashes.

The two of us were able to curb the Vietcong fire to some degree as the slicks scrambled out of the LZ in all directions, some with troops, many without, all taking fire as they fled. The mortars had stopped, but sporadic automatic-weapons fire continued and a .50 caliber machine-gun nest on the north side of the LZ was murderously effective. Three helicopters were wrecked, and three-quarters of the assault team were still pinned down in the LZ, which was strewn with dead and wounded.

I called the slick leader, and he confirmed that five of his birds got out without damage and were empty.

"Okay, we gotta get our troops out of the LZ before dark or they're in serious trouble. I think you can carry what's left," I told him.

"Unless you can knock out those gunners, and especially the .50s, I'm not gonna take my guys back in there, T-Bird 4," he replied.

"I understand. The Vikings just arrived and are attacking the gun positions as we speak," I replied, watching the Viking gunships make their firing runs on the enemy positions.

"Okay, T-Bird 4, we'll orbit here and wait for your call. We're about five miles south at 1,500 feet," informed the slick leader.

While the Vikings were attacking, I finally managed to get in radio contact with the ground commander. I told him he'd better get his troops to return fire on the enemy LZ perimeter positions if he wanted to get out of there alive. That got his attention, and they got an attack going.

The Viking team had fired rockets and machine gunned the enemy treeline positions but were unable to take out the .50 calibers. I knew that I couldn't extract the remaining troops and our crews without additional casualties if the .50-caliber position wasn't eliminated. I was low on ammo and fuel, but that .50-caliber position had to be taken out.

"Viking lead from T-Bird 4, I'm gonna climb up and make a high-angle rocket attack on the .50s. I can get a better shot that way. I'll call you when I'm in position, and I'd like you to make a simultaneous low-level diversionary attack."

"T-Bird 4, from Viking, we'll try to distract them, but if they catch you coming in like that, you're gonna take a beating."

"Yeah, I know. But we're running out of time, Viking."

"Roger. Call when you want me to go, T-Bird 4."

"Will do. You copy, T-Bird 8?"

"Copy lead. I'm with you, but I don't have any rockets left."

"Okay, T-Bird 8. I've got six remaining. That will have to do it. You cover me with machine-gun fire, and when I fire the rockets, break fast."

"Roger, let's go."

When I reached 1,500 feet above the jungle, I moved into position and asked the Viking lead to begin his attack on the .50-caliber position. The Vietcong began firing at the Viking gunships as I nosed over and started down. I was well into the diving run before I realized there were multiple .50s in the emplacement and a nest of automatic weapons.

I had made a major miscalculation, but I was committed. Red tracers the size of baseballs were coming straight at me. My copilot began firing the machine guns and so did my cabin gunners as I put my rocket sight on the muzzle flashes and fired a pair of rockets. I missed, hitting high. I edged the nose down more and fired another pair of rockets. High again. Damn! Now I could see the faces of the Vietcong gunners, and I knew I was gaining too much speed and getting too close to the enemy position. But I had no choice. I either hit that gun emplacement with my last two rockets or the game was over, and we were going home in body bags.

I pushed the cyclic forward even more, dropping the nose of the helicopter to keep the rocket sight on the target. Suddenly the windshield exploded on the copilot's side. "I'm hit!" he screamed.

The helicopter began to vibrate violently and the cockpit filled with smoke. I couldn't see my instruments, the rocket sight was useless, and I could hardly hold the controls.

"We're on fire, and we're taking hits," shouted the crew chief as the vibrations increased.

I didn't know it at the time but my gunner, who had been hanging outside the helicopter on a "monkey strap" so that he could shoot better, took a hit in his protective chest plate that knocked him clear back into the cabin of the helicopter.

I had to take out those .50 calibers! I was less than 500 feet above the Vietcong guns when I fired my last pair of rockets and pulled off in a hard right bank that made the helicopter shake so bad I nearly lost control.

"You got 'em, T-Bird 4! You got a direct hit!" I heard somebody shout over the radio as I struggled for control of the helicopter.

After leveling out and reducing power, the vibrations eased off and I regained control. I was relieved when I realized what had caused the violent vibration: retreating blade stall, which had been the result of my exceeding the helicopter's maximum airspeed in the steep dive.

"Where's the fire?" I quickly asked over the intercom.

"We put it out. It was a smoke grenade that took a hit," answered the crew chief.

I breathed another sigh of relief and glanced across at my copilot. He was wiping blood off his face. But it wasn't a bullet wound. It was cuts from plexiglass fragments when the windshield was shot out.

"Anybody else hurt?" I asked and got negative answers, except our gunner who was hurting from the blow of a .50-caliber round striking his armor plate.

"T-Bird 4, this is Viking lead. Man, I didn't think you were gonna pull out of that dive."

"I didn't either, Viking," I muttered.

"Good job, T-Bird. It's all quiet here now."

"Thanks for the help, Viking," I replied, then called the slicks and told them the LZ was clear for troop extraction.

I climbed to 1,000 feet and assessed our condition. Both T-Birds had sustained extensive damage. We were full of bullet holes, but the engine and transmission gauges looked good. Both birds were flying rough from damaged rotor blades, but they would get us home.

The downed helicopter crews and remaining troops were cleared from the LZ with no further casualties. The dead Vietnamese troops and the three downed helicopters were left behind. An operation would be initiated the next day to recover the bodies and helicopters, but it was not likely that much would be left.

As we headed for Soc Trang, I turned the controls over to the copilot and took a moment to reflect on the day. The sun was setting. It had been a long, damn day. I was tired, hungry, and, if I thought about it, scared. I wondered how many times I could survive this shit. Okay, no more reflections. It wasn't healthy. It's the game. Today I won.

Bill Kirk did beat the game. He completed more than three hundred combat sorties in Vietnam, came home, finished college, and flew helicopters in many civil operations. We were together at Hughes and McDonnell Douglas Helicopters for many years, and he is now regional sales manager at Agusta Aerospace Corporation.

11

Linda Morelli: Helicopter Pilot

The helicopter-instructor pilot, wearing a green ball cap with tufts of gray hair sticking out from under it, walked up to the bulletin board and looked at the list of new students for the Army Helicopter Primary Flight Training Center, Fort Rucker, Alabama. "Linda Morelli? Jesus, I hope that's a mistake," he muttered aloud.

"Whatta you hope is a mistake?" asked another helicopter-instructor pilot.

"One of my new students is listed as 'Linda.'"

"It ain't likely that Linda is a guy's name, even in 1980. You got yourself a female student."

"I can't believe they did this to me."

"Hey, they got no choice. The Army says we're gonna be training more females. I hear there will be two in our next class."

"I know, but why me?"

"I guess you drew the short straw. But that's just the way it is nowadays."

"Yeah, and the Army is goin' to Hell in a handbasket."

"Could be. But one thing's for sure, there's gonna be females in that handbasket, whether we like it or not."

"Something else is for sure."

"What?"

"I don't like it. And I'd be willing to bet that Linda Morelli is a cute little fluff with two left feet who couldn't put in a lightbulb without help."

April 7, 1980 (six weeks later)

Without a bobble, the TH-55 Army primary helicopter trainer lifted up from its marked spot on the tarmac at Hanchey Army Airfield, Fort Rucker, Alabama. It established a rock-steady hover for a moment, made a clearing turn, and then took off into forward flight.

The two helicopter instructors standing on the edge of the tarmac watched as the helicopter banked around, climbed up to traffic-pattern altitude, and entered the downwind leg. They kept their eyes focused on the "Mattel Messerschmitt," as the primary trainer was dubbed, until it had turned onto final approach and "slid down the string." Establishing a stable hover, the TH-55 then settled down onto the exact spot it had departed from.

"How was that for a perfect solo flight?" exclaimed the smiling instructor pilot wearing a green ball cap, with tufts of gray hair sticking out from under it.

The other instructor grinned. "Yeah, that cute little fluff, with the two left feet, who couldn't put in a lightbulb without help, is probably the best student in the class."

A big smile. "Yeah. Well, how was I to know that she would have natural coordination, a great attitude, study hard, and be as sharp as a tack? Huh? How was I supposed to know all that?"

June 10, 1980 (eight weeks later)

The big, turbine-powered Army UH-1H helicopter settled onto the tarmac at Fort Rucker. After two minutes of engine cooldown, the student pilot, Lt. Linda Morelli, twisted the throttle to the off position.

"I want to see you in the briefing room, Morelli," snapped the captain, who pulled off his flight helmet, climbed out of the helicopter, and walked off across the parking ramp without a backward glance.

As she completed the shutdown procedure, Linda Morelli ran back through the flight sequence in her mind. She had performed all of the maneuvers without incident and, as far as she could tell, without a major mistake. The captain, a check pilot, had made a few comments but said nothing critical about the flight. So what had she done wrong?

She knew he was upset about something. Or was it just the same old story—the usual male resentment of a woman intruding into a man's world? Well, she'd been through all that a thousand times, hadn't she? Yes, and it really didn't bother her that much any more. She had learned long ago to cope by just ignoring it and working harder.

Lt. Linda Morelli at awards ceremony, Fort Benning, Georgia, October 1977. (Courtesy Linda Morelli)

When she had first started the primary-training phase in the TH-55, her instructor had been cool and distant, his objection to her being there evident. And, in a way, she understood that. All the primary instructors were older, retired officers and warrant officers hired by the civilian primary-training contractor because of their experience. Their resentment of female intrusion was rooted in long-held traditions of the old military.

But after she had displayed an aptitude and a driving desire to succeed by listening, studying, and working hard, Morelli's instructor, who was old enough to be her father, had changed his attitude completely. And when she soloed, he was as proud of her as if she was indeed his own daughter.

But now that she was in the advanced phase of training, the tough nuts to crack were the regular Army instructors who didn't disguise their resentment of a female, particularly since she was a National Guard female. Even worse was the fact that the other regular Army male students resented her as much as the instructors, or even more so. It seemed that she had to prove to every instructor and every male classmate that she hadn't been selected for flight training because she was a cute little female token from some National Guard outfit filling a quota. She was there because she was qualified and could do the job.

Lt. Linda Morelli checking preflight procedures at Arizona National Guard, Phoenix, 1981. (Courtesy Linda Morelli)

To prove that, Linda had spent many extra hours studying, flying the simulators, and memorizing procedures and instrument limitations so that she could perform unerringly and respond without hesitation.

When Linda entered the briefing room a few minutes later, the ambient sound of voices decreased suddenly and the eyes of male students and instructors focused on her disapprovingly for a moment, then turned away contemptuously. She walked across the room to the table where the captain sat waiting for her. She could tell by the grim look on his face that this debriefing was not going to be good. He took a sip from his coffee cup and looked at her as she sat down opposite him. "My official comment is that you passed your check ride satisfactorily."

Linda was tongue-tied for a moment, then broke into a smile she couldn't contain. "Thank you, sir," she said.

"I haven't finished, lieutenant."

"Oh . . . yes, sir." Her smile dissolved.

"I'm going to level with you, Morelli. I would have flunked you in a New York second if I could have. But, I'm sorry to say, I couldn't find anything wrong with your flying. You obviously know the procedures, and you have good control touch. Now, I want to ask you an unofficial question."

"Yes, sir."

"What are you doing here?"

"What?"

"Why are you here?"

"I would think that is obvious, captain."

"It's not obvious to me, nor to anyone else around here. Just what are you trying to prove?"

"That I have the right stuff to become an Army National Guard helicopter pilot, regardless of my gender. That's what I'm going to prove, captain."

The captain hesitated and narrowed his eyes. "You've got the right stuff all right, Morelli. But it's misdirected. You're talented and you're smart. There's all kinds of things you could do in many fields and really make a contribution. Why do you have to pick something where all you're going to accomplish is disruption and resentment?"

"The disruption and the resentment is not my fault."

"Yes, it is. By just being here, it's your fault. This is a man's business, and your very presence is highly disruptive. You're a female and, I might say, a pretty one. That alone is distracting, not to mention the dissension caused by jealous wives. The politicians can decree unisex all they want, they aren't going to change human nature."

"That's reactionary reasoning, captain. This is 1980, remember? Women are going to enter any profession they can qualify for. And, I believe, do as good a job as a male. I am qualified for this training, and I want to become a helicopter pilot."

"Yeah, sure. Just what gave you those qualifications? I'll bet there were plenty of male applicants who were passed over so your guard unit could be politically correct and send a female."

"Not true!" flared Linda. "I went through a comprehensive selection process in the Delaware National Guard before being chosen as the best candidate to attend Army helicopter training."

"Sure you did."

Linda looked at the captain. Yes. It was the same old attitude. "So, what are you suggesting, captain? That I just up and quit?"

The captain nodded. "It would be in everyone's best interest, particularly the Army's."

"I disagree. And let me assure you that I'm not about to quit. I was taught at an early age that you don't ever give up and walk away from an unfinished task."

"That's admirable, but this is a task you shouldn't have begun in the first place."

"Not so. My grandparents immigrated from Italy to find a better life in a country where opportunity abounds for those who will apply themselves. The opportunity to fly an Army helicopter may not have been available to my grandmother, but it is to me, and I'm going to take it."

"Regardless of the consequences?"

"I don't see the consequences as you do. And even if I should quit, what are you going to say to all those females coming after me?"

"I'll say the same thing: 'You don't belong here. There are simply certain military functions that are men's domain, and females should stay out.'"

"Like helicopters and airborne?"

The captain paused a moment, then nodded, and took a sip of his coffee.

"It might surprise you to know that I completed Army airborne training at Fort Benning, Georgia, three years ago and got my jump wings."

"You did?" said the captain, with an incredulous look on his face. "You graduated from jump school?"

"Yes, and I have since made numerous operational jumps at Fort Bragg and in the Canal Zone."

The captain looked at the lieutenant with an open mouth.

"And I can assure you that is the male bastion of all Army schools."

The captain cleared his throat. "Yeah, I . . . know."

"I'm not saying that qualifies me for helicopter training, but it substantiates that I can measure up under demanding conditions, whatever they are. And I believe my record here at Fort Rucker substantiates that too, does it not, captain?"

"Yes . . . it does. I had no idea that you . . ."

"I would be the first to agree that if a female can't cut the mustard, then she should be disqualified in the same manner a male student would, but you have to give us a chance, and you and your contemporaries are not, because you're prejudiced."

"I don't consider myself prejudiced, lieutenant. I'm thinking of the best interests of the Army."

"You may think you are, but you're not just thinking of the Army. You just told me I passed my check ride and I fly well. Right?"

The captain nodded.

"And isn't that what the Army wants?"

The captain shifted in his chair.

"Pardon me?"

The captain looked up at the lieutenant and grinned. "Yeah, that's what they want, and you do it well. And you do something else well—you sure put up a good argument."

"Thank you, sir."

The captain got up from the briefing table and said, "Lieutenant Morelli, could I buy you a beer at the Officers Club?"

The pretty girl with the brown hair and blue eyes smiled and said, "Yes, you sure may, captain."

Linda Morelli was one of the first females to complete Army helicopter training, receiving her silver wings in November 1980 at Fort Rucker, Alabama. She is also one of the first, if not the first, female to earn both Army airborne jump wings and pilot wings. She went on to fly helicopters in the National Guard in Delaware, Arizona, and California until her retirement in February 1996 as a major. She flew many different models of helicopters under various operational conditions, always excelling in her performance. On May 1, 1994, Linda was sworn in as a deputy sheriff of Riverside, California, and began another career as one of a handful of female pilots in the United States who fly law enforcement helicopters.

12

Secret of Hog Back Canyon

It was late afternoon before I could get away from my Washington, D.C., office and head for National Airport in Virginia. The traffic was its usual bumper-to-bumper crawl across the Fourteenth Street Bridge. By the time I finally got to the airport, parked my car, and walked to the general aviation terminal, the sun was low on the western horizon.

I didn't like starting a flight over the Allegheny Mountains that late in the day because there was usually afternoon thunderstorms that time of year. But the weather forecaster said there was only a 30 percent chance of encountering one on my flight to West Virginia, and, since I had an important sales call in Charleston the next day, I decided to go.

I completed a preflight check of my sleek jet helicopter, cranked it up, and called Washington control tower for takeoff clearance. The tower operator gave me a departure clearance for helicopter route one, and I took off and headed up the Potomac River.

My concern about the weather was quickly forgotten as I skimmed over Memorial Bridge and saw the glistening marble columns of the Kennedy Center and the Lincoln Memorial shimmering in the late-afternoon sun. Of course, my spirits always escalate when I slip the surly bonds of earth in the helicopter. It's like stepping through a magic door into another world, where you can observe the passing parade of life below, yet you're free of its congestion and anxieties.

The route I was flying is a low-altitude corridor for helicopter traffic entering or departing the Washington, D.C., area west. It follows the path of the Potomac River that winds alongside the George Washington Parkway. Airplane traffic follows the same route, but at a much higher altitude. They can't enjoy the beautiful river landscape, the lush foliage, the magnificent homes, and the colorful sights along the Chesapeake and the Ohio Canal.

"Helicopter zero zero fox, Washington tower. Traffic at twelve o'clock," snapped the voice in my earphones, reminding me that I did, however, share the corridor with other helicopters—a lot of them—a far cry from my early days in the Air Force when I was the only helicopter in Washington.

"Roger tower, zero zero fox is looking," I quickly responded.

I spotted the traffic a second or two later. It was an Army chopper headed down the river toward the Pentagon. Nowadays there was a steady stream of helicopters going in and out of the Pentagon heliport—another far cry from the days when it was a no no to even go near the place. I rolled in a little right bank and keyed the mike: "Got the traffic, Wash tower."

A couple of minutes later I zipped across the Cabin John Bridge (now called American Legion Bridge), the exit point of helicopter route one, and headed west. I was now flying over Virginia's beautiful "hunt country" with its green, gentle rolling hills laced with white-washed fences and sprawling estates. I could see a few trainers working their thoroughbred horses in manicured pastures or on private racetracks. On one estate I saw a competitor's helicopter parked in the front yard: a Bell 206. I smiled to myself. Even if I didn't sell him the helicopter, it showed the guy who lived there had imagination. In the helicopter-sales business, you win some and lose some.

By the time the rolling hills gave way to the first ridges of the Allegheny, the sun had dipped below the horizon and darkness was quickly settling. I put the bird into a climb and scanned the darkening skies ahead. There were no storm clouds in sight. But, since I knew that could change quickly, I climbed up above the mountains, and set a direct course to Charleston.

Normally, I like to fly low, pointing the nose of my bird at whatever looks interesting up ahead. You can do that in a helicopter because you can always drop down and look at a road sign if you get lost, or check in at the nearest motel. However, flying over mountains after dark, with the threat of thunderstorms, is another story.

Sure enough, about twenty minutes later, I saw a flash of lightning directly ahead. "So much for the three-to-one odds," I muttered to myself as I watched the stars disappear into a huge black shape that suddenly blocked my flight route. Those of us who have been caught in a thunderstorm don't go back for seconds; and I didn't intend to now. My plan was to stay on course until it began to get rough, then start my detour. I wasn't sure I could get around this big "mamoo," because it looked widespread and mean. And, as I got closer, the lightning charges grew intense and more frequent.

About the same time that a voice in my head told me to turn around and get out of there, the helicopter was slammed by a sudden wind gust that spun it around in a wild, gyrating arch, literally swapping ends and pitching like a bucking bronco. I fought for control as lightning flashed all around me and torrential rain beat the aluminum sides of the helicopter mercilessly.

I knew I had screwed up and got too close to the cell of the thunderstorm. It had engulfed me in its vicious wind currents, and now I had no choice but to get on the ground as soon as possible. But that's one of the great advantages of the whirlybird: it doesn't need a landing field. If you get yourself into a bad situation, you can always land.

I glanced down just as a flash of lightning illuminated the earth below. It wasn't a pretty sight. I was over a rugged section of the West Virginia mountains with high, narrow ridges and deep, wooded canyons that twisted and turned in never-ending, convoluted patterns. But there was no alternative. I had to land. I lowered the collective and started down into what looked like the bottom of an inkwell. It was, indeed, like riding a bucking bronco as I wrestled to keep my erratic flight path between two mountain ridges that loomed as darkened shapes in my peripheral vision.

I turned on the landing light, slowed my forward speed, and started a steep approach into the blackness. The heavy rain glared off the light, making it difficult to see. But fortunately, a brilliant bolt of lightning flashed, illuminating a huge oak tree directly below. I kicked rudder pedal, swung off to one side, and dropped down into a narrow opening between two other trees.

I quickly shut off the engine and braked the rotor blades to a stop, then sat there staring into the blackness and listening to my pounding heart above the roar of the rain on the canopy. The thunderstorm must have been directly over me by then as the wind was buffeting the helicopter violently, and one bolt of lightning after another illuminated the dancing tree branches all around me.

I'd been caught in thunderstorms before, but not at night over mountains. And this baby was a ripper. The rain was pounding the helicopter cabin with such force that it was coming right through the door facing into the cockpit. We sales-demonstration pilots at Hughes Helicopter Company were always fussing at the engineers about rain leaking through the doors. I don't think, however, that any door could have resisted that deluge.

A booming thunderclap jolted my frayed nerves and reminded me that this thunderstorm could keep me right there in the wilderness for the remainder of the night. I didn't like the prospect of that, but then I deserved whatever I got for being overconfident and letting myself get caught that way. On the other hand, the storm could pass over in an hour or so and there should be clear skies behind it. If so, I could still get to Charleston tonight.

I retrieved my jacket from the backseat and settled into the most comfortable position I could manage to wait for the thunderstorm to do its thing. I'd been looking through the water-streaked canopy at the raging storm, flinching with each thunderclap, when suddenly a figure appeared directly in front of the helicopter. The image was only there a second or two before dissolving as the lightning flash faded.

I sat up in the seat and stared into the darkness. Had I really seen someone? Or was it my imagination? Probably just the tree branches in front of the helicopter. No . . . I was certain I'd seen something other than tree branches. I watched intently, waiting for the next lightning flash, which now that I wanted it, seemed to never come.

Actually, it couldn't have been more than a few seconds later when the next lightning bolt came, and there she was—a young girl in a long, white dress—standing directly in front of the helicopter. The illumination was so intense that she appeared suspended in a shimmering halo, with the rain cascading her long blond hair down over her shoulders.

She was real! And she was standing so close to the helicopter that if not for the canopy I could have reached out and touched her. She stood motionless, her arms at her sides, with the wind whipping the dress against her tall, slender frame. Despite the flood of rainwater pouring over her face, our eyes met, and, suddenly, I had the bizarre feeling that she was trying to send me some kind of telepathic message. Then she began to dissolve into darkness as the illumination from the lightning receded.

I stared into the darkness, waiting anxiously for the next lightning flash. When it came a few seconds later, she was gone. All I saw now was the pouring rain and dancing tree branches.

How could she have disappeared so quickly?

I unlatched the door and swung out of the cockpit into the rain. I saw nothing more than I had from inside the helicopter, and I was instantly drenched. I quickly retreated back into the cockpit and shut the door just as another lightning flash illuminated the world outside. But nothing had changed. The rain poured, the thunder roared, and the wind lashed the tree branches. There was no trace of the girl in the white dress.

After I sat in the cockpit for awhile, I began to wonder if perhaps the emotion of that earlier bout with the thunderstorm had upset my internal stability system and sparked my imagination a little. I mean a little more than usual. Everybody knows that all pilots are prone to wild imaginations, particularly helicopter pilots.

As it often does in a thunderstorm, the wind and rain suddenly stopped. I dug out my flashlight and climbed out of the helicopter. It was strangely quiet now. The only sound was the rainwater dripping from the leaves and an occasional rumble of thunder off in the distance. I searched the area around the helicopter but could find no trace of the girl. Had I really seen her? I wondered, as I stood in the dripping darkness, shining the flashlight around the clearing. I glanced at the narrow corridor in the trees that I'd traversed on my landing. I realized that it had been another one of those times when my guardian angel was watching over me.

My guardian angel?

The girl in the white dress?

Now my imagination was really working.

Come on, Richard, be realistic.

But . . . she was there . . . I saw her!

Did you really?

Yes, I saw her, all right. But she's obviously someone who lived around there. She heard the helicopter and was curious. That's all. . . . Right?

Of course, that's all.

I snapped off the flashlight and let my eyes adjust to the darkness. I could see stars shining through the trees. That meant the thunderstorm had passed over, and I could get to Charleston. It was going to be a squeaker climbing out of there in the darkness. Well, I'd flown down through that narrow passage, so what comes down can go up, especially the bird I was flying. It could get in and out of tight places, because of its small rotor size.

In the world of helicopters, at that time, there were two basic types of civil helicopters. One type had a single, teetering rotor blade; the other, articulated, multirotor blades. Each has advantages and disadvantages. My bird had five rotor blades, which in this instance was an advantage because of its small rotor diameter.

I looked at the corridor again. Yeah, I could climb out through that all right and fly to Charleston in time for dinner.

But I had seen her. No question about it.

Do helicopter guardian angels wear white dresses?

Richard, get in the helicopter and go.

As I started to climb in, something caught my eye: a tiny speck of light coming through a clump of branches. I walked over to an opening in the foliage and looked. Although pale and distant, it was sure enough a light. In a strange way, I felt a touch of disappointment. The light probably came from a nearby house, where the girl in the white dress lived.

I knew all along she was a real girl.

Of course you did.

People lived out in that wilderness country. "Homesteaders" and "mountain people," they called them. I know, because I'd flown over many a lone cabin in isolated sections of the Allegheny Mountains.

Well, that solved the mystery, and I needed to get on to Charleston. I was wet, cold, and hungry.

The house with the light couldn't be that far away.

And then I'd know for sure.

I already knew for sure.

No you don't.

Curiosity killed the cat.

I started to climb into the helicopter, then hesitated . . . But I've got to know.

I snapped on the flashlight and started down what appeared to be a trail in the general direction of the light. It was pitch black, and my flashlight was one of those little jobs that don't put out much light, so I collided with a lot of wet bushes and tree branches.

By the time I came out of the woods and into what appeared to be a meadow, my curiosity was peaked. And everybody also knows that in addition to wild imaginations, helicopter pilots are notoriously curious.

It was a meadow all right, and, as I sloshed through it, I remembered that I was wearing a new pair of shoes. The light, although dim, was plain to see now, and, by the time I crossed the meadow, I could tell that it was coming from a lone window in a darkened structure set back in the trees. I continued and walked into a barbed-wire fence without seeing it, cut my hand, and dropped the flashlight. Naturally it went out. After a couple of superlatives, I found it in the grass and, fortunately, it still worked. I managed to get through the barbed-wire fence and, a couple minutes later, was standing in front of the house.

I couldn't see much except a dull, yellowish glow through the window—probably a kerosine lamp. The window was back under a steep roof, which I could tell was rusted, corrugated iron.

As I hesitated there in the darkness, it suddenly dawned on me that even though this was wilderness, I was trespassing on someone's private property in the middle of the night for no reason other than my curiosity.

While I was trying to dispel my sudden apprehension, the flashlight went out. Now it would be difficult to find my way back to the helicopter, and, after all, this was sort of an emergency. My rationale was enough to send me on.

I stumbled up the stone steps in the darkness and knocked on what I assumed was the front door.

I could hear instant shuffling and movement inside the house. Then, I was certain I heard the cocking of a rifle or shotgun. I'd been shot at before in World War II and Korea, and I didn't want any more of that. So I was on the verge of retreat, when the door squeaked open and there stood a little eight- or nine-year-old boy, carrying a kerosene lantern. It was such a surprise, I just stared at him for a moment.

"Hello there," I finally said.

"Hello," he answered in a clear voice, looking at me curiously with big round eyes.

He was barefoot, wearing threadbare bib overalls that were too short and hung halfway up his shin bone. His hair was long and looked like sun-ripened wheat, parted right down the middle.

"Uh, are your parents home, son?" I asked.

His eyes deflected.

I caught a glimpse of movement behind him. The door was only partially open, so I couldn't see much inside the house. But I did see a door closing in the rear of the room where a hanging kerosene lamp cast dull, yellow light over walls that were plastered with faded magazine pictures. There were no other persons visible, but I knew someone was there as I could sense their eyes on me—probably over the sights of a gun.

"I'm a helicopter pilot. I got caught in that thunderstorm and had to land," I explained nervously, but in a loud enough voice that the hidden eyes could hear, and be assured that I came in peace.

The little boy nodded politely.

I was surprised at his composure. Generally, kids are curious over the helicopter. "Are your parents, or someone else, at home?" I tried again.

"Canyonville is jest over thet ridge," he said, again avoiding my question. It was evident he didn't want to lie, but he also wasn't going to give me any information. I'd heard that these mountain folk were pretty aloof and wary of strangers.

"Canyonville? Is that a town?"

He nodded.

"Just over the ridge?"

He nodded again.

"The ridge north?"

"Nor west," he corrected.

I nodded.

"They got a hotel over there." He spoke clearly, but with a heavy accent.

"A hotel?"

He nodded. "Miz Haney's Hotel," he added then stepped back as though to close the door.

"Uh, son, do you have a sister?" I asked quickly.

He hesitated, then shook his head.

"A girl . . . a girl in a white dress came out to my helicopter."

He shook his head again, then sort of nodded, as though to bid me adieu, and gently closed the door.

I stood in the darkness, wondering what I should do next. It was evident the elders in that house did not want to address me in any way. The little boy was their spokesman, and he'd said all there was to say, with hospitality limited to information on where I could find a hotel. In a way, I couldn't blame them. After all, I was just a stranger in the night.

But I had a gnawing feeling that it was something more than that—something to do with the girl.

I decided I'd better forget about her, for the time being anyway, and figure out how I was going to find my way back to the helicopter. Or should I knock on the door again and demand to speak to an adult? My id, or something, told me that that was not a good plan. I pulled out the flashlight and shook it. It came on. That seemed to validate my inclination to get out of there. When I got back to the helicopter, I couldn't help look around one more time for some trace of the girl. There wasn't any, and I was getting so cold my teeth were chattering, so I made one last survey of the corridor in the trees I'd have to fly through and climbed into the helicopter.

As soon as I got the engine started, I turned on the heat. The Hughes engineers may not have designed rainproof doors, but they did themselves justice with the heater. It put out plenty of hot air and did it ever feel good. I just sat there awhile with the heater on full blast. I had dry clothes in my suitcase in the backseat, but it would be such a hassle to change, and I decided I could wait until I got to Charleston. When I got enough feeling back in my hands and feet to handle the controls, I revved up takeoff power, flipped on my landing light, and eased the helicopter up through the trees, and off into the night sky.

As always, I felt great as soon as I was airborne. It was still pitch black, but the stars were bright and the sky clear. When I cleared the ridge, I glanced down, and, sure enough, there was a little cluster of lights in the bottom of the next canyon. It had to be Canyonville.

I have always thought of the helicopter as akin to a magic carpet: you can go anywhere and, wherever you go, there is an adventure waiting. And since my curiosity was still running high, I was tempted to land down there in Canyonville. But, then I'd probably had enough adventure for one night, so I flipped on the radio and tuned in Charleston. Glancing down for one last look, I saw it: Miz Haney's Hotel! I was sure of it. I kicked rudder and rolled in cyclic for a descending turn. I couldn't help myself. All I could see was a dark shape beside the creek, but there was a lighted sign out front that read MIZ HANEY'S HOTEL.

No, don't land down there, Richard. Charleston's not more than a thirty-minute flight, and you can get a martini, a good dinner, and . . .

I went down on the collective and back on the cyclic in one swift movement and set up a steep approach to a clearing on the creek bank next to the hotel. I flipped on the landing light and checked for wires. It was clear, so I eased the chopper down into a hover and landed. It was just one of those things I couldn't help. My curiosity was back in command.

After I'd shut the helicopter down, I crawled out and walked up to the front of a large, old ramshackle house, where a heavyset woman with a mop of red hair and a tall, gangly youth were standing under a porch light, staring at me.

"You want a room?" she asked.

I hesitated. Did I want a room? Well, it didn't seem right to just drop out of the night sky and start asking questions about a girl in a white dress, so I said, "Do you have a vacancy?"

"Yeah, I got one."

"Is there somewhere I can get something to eat?"

"Sure. There's a bar and grill down the holler a ways. Ralph will drive ya over in the pickup."

Ralph nodded.

"I don't get too many *heelocopter* guests. But Charlie Bodrey thet flies the Mountain State Coal *heelocopter* spent the night here awhile back. He got caught in a thunderstorm too."

I nodded, wondering how she knew I'd been caught in the thunderstorm. Then I remembered that I was all wet.

"Can you pay cash? I don't take credit cards."

I nodded again.

"Good. Come on in an' register, and I'll show you your room. Ralph, go get the pickup and bring it around front."

Ralph grunted, meandered off the porch, and disappeared into the darkness.

"You got a telephone?" I asked, after I'd retrieved my suitcase from the helicopter. I needed to call flight service and cancel my flight plan. I was already overdue.

"Yep. Got one, but it don't always work," she said as we entered the house.

Miz Haney's Hotel had creaking wood floors and peeling wallpaper. But it was warm inside, and the telephone worked, so I closed my flight plan.

"That *heelocopter* must leak pretty bad, huh?" she said, watching me fill out the registration card.

"Only when it rains," I said.

She nodded. "Charlie said the same thing."

"By the way, do you happen to know the people who live just over the ridge to the south of here?" I asked, handing her the registration card.

The big woman seemed to hesitate. "I know just about everybody around here. You mean over in Hog Back Canyon?"

"I guess. It's a house with a corrugated iron roof beside a meadow."

She nodded. "I know them. Why do you ask?"

"Oh . . . I got caught in that thunderstorm and had to land over there."

"Yeah?"

"Well, I was just curious. Do they have a tall girl with long blond hair?"

She hesitated, looked at me suspiciously for a moment, and then said, "They have three boys."

"Only boys?"

"Yeah."

"Uh, is there a young girl living there?"

"No."

"Is there another family in that area?"

"No. They're the only ones live in that canyon."

"Well, how close is their nearest neighbor?"

"A long way. Not many folks go over there, cause ya gotta walk or ride a horse. There ain't no road."

I shrugged. "Well, I saw a young girl over there during the storm. She was wearing a white dress."

Miz Haney frowned. "You musta been seeing things."

I shook my head. "I saw her, all right."

"Sometimes all that lightning and thunder in those big thunderstorms will play tricks with your head," said Miz Haney, handing me one of those old-fashioned skeleton door keys. "Your room is at the top of the stairs on the left. Bathroom two doors down. It takes a little while for the hot water to come."

As I changed my clothes, I tried to rationalize what Miz Haney had told me. I don't like thunderstorms, but they don't play tricks with my head. I know what I saw. But I had to admit, I had no answer . . . except that I sensed by her reaction that she knew more than she was telling about the family in Hog Back Canyon. . . . Or was that just more of my overactive imagination?

Ralph drove the pickup right down the middle of the narrow blacktop that wound along the bottom of the canyon beside the creek. Fortunately no cars came the other way and we made it to Blackie's Bar and Grill alive. It was less than a mile from the hotel, so in the interest of self-preservation, I told Ralph I would walk back to the hotel after I had dinner.

The back side of Blackie's stuck out over the creek on stilts and the front side was on dirt dug out of the mountain. Pickup trucks were parked every which way, with some sticking out onto the roadway. A green and red neon beer sign glowed in the front window, and I could tell by the sound that the place was jumping. But when I walked in everything stopped, even the jukebox.

Tables were placed about the room with the bar stretching across the entire back end. There was a jukebox and a small dance floor on one side and a pool table on the other. The place was packed, and every eye there was focused on me. I kind of smiled and headed for an empty stool at the bar.

A new song started on the jukebox, and the sound level rose again as everyone picked up were they'd left off. While I waited for the bartender, I looked around and noticed that for the most part it was a young group, and I could tell by their dress that they were coal workers and their girlfriends—pretty girls and handsome young men laughing and talking, and of course, flirting and sparring.

The bartender had gray hair and deep lifelines on his weathered face. He busied himself at the other end of the bar for awhile and then moseyed down to where I sat. I ordered a dry martini on the rocks. He raised an eyebrow, then went to work fixing it.

"Am I too late to get something to eat?" I asked, when he returned with the mart.

"No, Alice stays back there till eleven. Whatta ya want?"

"Well, uh . . . whatta ya got?"

"Everybody around here knows what we got, so we don't have no menu."

I smiled. "Well, can Alice fix me a steak?"

"Sure. How do you like it?"

"How about medium?"

"Medium it is."

"Sounds great. I'm starved," I said, taking a big gulp of the mart.

He nodded and, sticking his head through a little window at the back of the bar, shouted, "One steak, medium!"

A couple of minutes later he returned and said, "How's the martini?"

"It's perfect," I replied, because surprisingly it was.

"Don't get much call for those. Most folks around here drink beer."

"I noticed that."

"You just passin' through?"

"Yeah. You might say that. You live here long?"

"Yep. I worked in the coal mines with John L. Lewis. That's before your time."

"You have been around for awhile. I guess you know everybody around here."

"That I do."

Now was the time, so I said, "You know a family that lives on the other side of the ridge to the south?"

He hesitated. "You mean in Hog Back Canyon?"

I nodded.

He hesitated again. "Yeah, I know them. Why do you ask?"

Strange. That was the same question Miz Haney had asked . . . or was I becoming paranoid over this whole thing? "Oh, no special reason. I just wondered if you knew them."

He leaned against the bar in front of me as though to emphasize what he was going to say: "They are mountain folks and good Christians."

"Uh, I'm sure they are," I replied.

About that time someone shouted for a beer, and he went down to the other end of the bar.

A few minutes later, Alice passed my steak out through the little window. I had just started wolfing it down when the guy sitting next to me fell off his stool. Everyone laughed and his buddies scooped him up, carried him outside, and dumped him in the back of their pickup, and the party went on.

When I finished the steak, the bartender returned and asked did I want anything else. I said no and while he was figuring out what I owed him, I decided to ask one last question about the mystery girl. "That family over in Hog Back Canyon, they have a tall blond girl, don't they?"

He looked at me strangely; at least it seemed to me that he was. Finally he said, "No. They don't have no girls."

I thought about all this on the walk back to the hotel. In reality it was a simple incident, and I was probably making a mountain out of a molehill, as the old saying goes. But I couldn't get it out of my thoughts. I was confident I'd seen the girl, and she had to have been a member of that family since no one else lived over there. . . . So why had Mrs. Haney and the bartender denied her existence? What strange set of circumstances would prompt them to do that? It was evident to me they both had avoided the true story. What was the secret of Hog Back Canyon? . . . Or was the whole thing, indeed, a product of my imagination? . . . No. Not really. . . . Then perhaps she was my guardian angel. . . . Come on, Richard.

I had trouble sleeping that night, even though Miz Haney's Hotel bed had one of those old-fashioned feather mattresses. And when I did drop off, my dreams were all mixed up with flashing scenes of the girl in the white dress. When my travel alarm rung at six o'clock, I was still sleepy, so I turned it off and went into a sound sleep.

It was midmorning of a beautiful day when I finally got up, dressed, and went out to the helicopter. Breakfast was supposed to come with the room, but Miz Haney and Ralph were nowhere to be seen, so I decided I'd get breakfast in Charleston.

A couple of curious spectators were watching the helicopter for me. I said hello and answered a couple of questions as I did my walk-around inspection. Then I climbed in, cranked her up, and lifted off the creek bank.

I climbed up and over the ridge to the south in a couple of minutes. After a slight bank to the west, I was above Hog Back Canyon, where I easily spotted the house by the meadow. I flew around the area for awhile, searching carefully, and found no evidence of any other inhabitants in the canyon. Satisfied, I swung back over the meadow, dropped the nose, and angled down so I could see the house plainly. I even spotted the barbed-wire fence and the grove of trees where I had landed the night before. I eased off on the collective and hovered slowly over the house. The only movement I saw was a few scurrying chickens. There was no other sign of life, but I knew those same hidden eyes were watching me.

Then I saw it! At one side of the house was a clothesline drawn between two trees. Hanging among the other clothes in the morning sun, was a long white dress. I smiled, there in the cockpit of my jet helicopter, then pulled pitch, banked around to the west, and headed for Charleston.

I sold quite a few helicopters in West Virginia, because it's ideal transportation for supervisory personnel in that mountain country. What would require hours in a pickup truck, on a winding road, can be done with the helicopter in a few minutes. And during the course of my sales activities and demonstration flights, I made a lot of friends and enjoyed many a great adventure in the "Mountain State." But certainly one of the most intriguing, and one that I still wonder about, is the "Secret of Hog Back Canyon."

13

Heli-Bits

"Slattery's Place," as I call it, might sound like the name of a quaint pub. It's not. But to a helicopter lover, it's even better than a quaint pub.

If you take the elevator to the third floor in the headquarters of the Helicopter Association International (HAI) in Alexandria, Virginia, turn left, and walk about thirty feet, you'll find yourself in a fascinating, miniature helicopter world. Over a period of thirty years John Slattery, the curator at the Helicopter Foundation International (HFI), has collected a model of just about every helicopter ever made. He has also collected and cataloged what is probably the most extensive helicopter archives in the world.

The HFI is a nonprofit foundation dedicated to the preservation and promotion of the history of the vertical-lift industry. It is housed by the HAI, a professional trade association for the civil helicopter industry. Its 1,400 member organizations and 1,300 individual members in seventy nations operate more the 4,000 helicopters, flying approximately 2 million hours annually. I had gone to the HFI for some research on a couple of the stories for this book, and I felt like a kid in a candy store. No matter what I asked for, "Slatts," as he's called around there, produced it for me.

As I transcribed the data, Slattery, who was a Nam vet and a helicopter pilot for many years, told me a great story that I just had to pass on. That gave me the idea of asking some of the other helicopter veterans around the country to give me their favorite "Heli-Bit." I did some editing and added some dialog where appropriate, but here are the stories pretty much as they were told to me.

"Bull Story" from John Slattery

It was a few days before Christmas 1960, or maybe 1961, when the USAF Special Mission Squadron at Bolling Air Force Base, Washington, D.C., got a call from Air Force Gen. Curtis LeMay's Pentagon office advising that the general wanted one of the executive-configured Bell UH-13J model helicopters made ready for him. For those who don't know who General LeMay was, military historians will tell you that, as commander of the Strategic Air Command, he was probably more responsible than any other any person for preventing a nuclear holocaust during the critical 1950s phase of the Cold War. He was also brilliant, demanding, and tough as nails.

At the time of this story, the general was Air Force Chief of Staff at the Pentagon, and the Special Mission Squadron was based just across the Potomac River at Bolling Air Force Base. The squadron's mission was to provide air transportation for Pentagon and top government officials, which included LeMay, who was top, and special.

But unlike the other specials, when the general wanted to go somewhere, he flew himself, even in the helicopter. He'd come over there one day and simply said he wanted to check out in a helicopter, so they cranked up a H-13G model Bell, and, after a few lessons, he was off and running.

Anyway, this day he showed up with a bunch of Christmas presents, loaded them into a J model Bell and took off for Arthur Godfrey's ranch over in Virginia's "Hunt Country," west of Leesburg. He and Godfrey were good friends and had even gone on an African safari together using a 47G model Bell to spot game. (Godfrey was a popular radio and TV personality of that era who had also learned to fly helicopters.)

As the story goes, Godfrey told LeMay to be sure and park his helicopter inside the fence next to the house. But not many folks told General LeMay what to do. He parked the J model outside the fence in the pasture. After they unloaded the Christmas packages and went inside, Godfrey's resident bull came plodding across the pasture. As he approached the helicopter, he apparently saw his reflection in the bubble. Naturally, he had to protect his turf from this intruder, and charged.

Later, when LeMay came out to his helicopter, it looked like it had run head on into a bulldozer. The bubble was broken out, and helicopter pieces were scattered all over the pasture where the bull stood, switching his tail, and looking proud of his handiwork.

"FIRST LOOP" FROM THE HFI FILES

In March 1949 the U.S. Navy and Frank Piasecki, president of the Piasecki Helicopter Company, jointly released this story, which previously had been classified.

During test flights aimed at demonstrating the high-performance XHJP-1 helicopter's ability to withstand high g forces, veteran test pilot Jim Ryan performed a perfect loop. The loop was witnessed by dozens of onlookers, including company officials and Navy inspectors who said they believed it was the first-ever recorded loop. A careful examination of the XHJP-1 showed no structural failures.

Jim Ryan often gave this off-the-record account:

> I had made two dive runs trying to get up to the required g-force test figures and couldn't quite make it. So I decided on my third run I was gonna really honk it, and I did. I pulled in all I could get and hit the g figures all right, but I also found myself going vertical with nothing but blue sky in the canopy.
>
> Instinct told me I was in trouble, and the only way I could see to get me and the bird out of it was to go on around. I'd heard most of the engineers say the helicopter couldn't be looped. But I was past the point of no return, so I just held pitch and cyclic, and to my surprise and relief she came on over like any other loop I'd ever made in fixed-wing aircraft. I got to admit, though, I was glad to see that old horizon come across the canopy as I came down on the back side of the loop.

Looping a helicopter in the early days was definitely a no-no. Most of today's high-tech helicopters can be looped, although it's not an approved maneuver and, therefore, not recommended.

"NIGHT MISSION" FROM KIETH DROEGEMEIER

I was looking out through the rain-streaked windshield, watching our homemade searchlight probe the raging sea below, when suddenly the fishing boat, bobbing like a cork, appeared out of the darkness. I thought: This is crazy. How in the world am I going to get those fishermen off that boat?

I was a helicopter pilot in Detachment Three of the USAF, 24th Helicopter Squadron, at Itazuke, Japan. Our mission was to support the construction and resupply of radar sites with the H-21 Piasecki "Work Horse" helicopter. We weren't in the rescue business, that was the responsibility of the 41st AARS Wing. But as we all know, when someone gets in trouble and calls on the nearest helicopter, you respond. That's what happened one night in November 1956, during a typhoon in northern Kyushu.

激浪に漂流12時間

空からナワはしご

三人救助 米軍ヘリコプターが活躍

drifting in raging waves for 12 hours.

a rope-ladder from the sky

the relief of three men; the activity of the helicopter (U.S.)

写真 夜の海上で空からの救助に活躍する米軍ヘリコプター

Captain Droegemeier (left)

Japanese newspaper story of Lt. Keith Droegemeier's night sea-rescue mission near Itazuke, Japan, November 1956. He was flying an Air Force H-21 Piasecki Helicopter. (Courtesy Kieth Droegemeier)

We received a call in the late afternoon that a small fishing boat was in distress off the island's northern coast, and, because of the high seas and gale-force winds, the Coast Guard had been unsuccessful in effecting a rescue. After we rigged up a handheld searchlight and found a rope ladder, my copilot, Lt. Albert Churcher, my crew chief, Airman Frank Linhart, and I cranked up an H-21 and took off into the darkness to see if we could help.

It was an awful night with pouring rain and vicious wind gusts that battered the Piasecki, making it difficult to control. We searched for some time before finally spotting the small, 40-foot boat. It was dead in the water and being blown toward the rocky shoreline where gigantic waves pounded the rocks. It was evident that if we couldn't get the fishermen off, they were doomed.

Maintaining a hover over the boat was like trying to keep a bucking bronco over one spot. In the rain-drenched doorway, my crew chief attempted to keep the homemade searchlight on the boat. My copilot, with his head out the side cockpit window, gave me instructions over the intercom. Three fishermen, clinging to the wallowing boat, would appear one moment and disappear the next, as huge waves sent sheets of spume over the deck.

"Left! . . . left! . . . forward! . . . forward! . . . right! . . . right! . . . hold!" came my copilot's instructions as we tried to get the swinging rope ladder where they could grab it.

Finally, one of the fishermen caught the rope ladder and began to climb up. I worried whether he could make it up the swinging ladder into the helicopter. He had some trouble, but he made it. The second fisherman also made it after a couple of tries. But now the boat was dangerously near the rocks, and there was one remaining fisherman.

I was exhausted from fighting the controls in the gusting winds for nearly forty-five minutes, and, despite the cold, perspiration dripped into my eyes. But I had to get that last fisherman. Adrenaline kicked in, and we snatched the last one off a few minutes later. With three very appreciative Japanese fisherman sitting on the aluminum floor of the H-21, I pulled pitch and headed back to base.

"A DRAMATIC LESSON" FROM WALT ZIMMERMAN

It was the winter of 1963, and I was assigned to Detachment 42, 44th AAR Squadron, at Dow Air Force Base, Maine. We'd had aircraft out all morning searching for a missing USAF F-101 "Voodoo" interceptor that had gone down the night before in a snowstorm. There had been no luck until word came that the radar observer, or "scope dope" as they were called in those days, had been found. I interviewed him when they brought him in, and he said he'd ejected from the aircraft after it went into an uncontrollable spin. He'd survived the night in the snow with the aid of his survival gear and walked to a road the next day, where a passing motorist picked him up.

He told me he'd seen the explosion of the doomed aircraft when it crashed not far from where he had landed in his parachute. I asked him if he could find the place he spent the night if we flew him to the area in a chopper. He said he could, so we crawled into a Kaman H-43 "Husky" and headed out there.

We found the place where he'd camped, and I was hovering over it when suddenly I realized I couldn't pull the cyclic stick aft. It was jammed in a neutral position, which meant I was going to have big trouble landing. It's a tall order to land a helicopter without aft cyclic control. And, as all helicopter pilots know, any control linkage problem is a potential catastrophe.

I called our field-search communication's center and asked them to have the state police block traffic on a three-lane highway that went up the mountainside nearby. Then I made like an airplane and flew the H-43 up the hill for a running landing. After I shut down and stopped the rotors, my crew chief unbuttoned the access panels and found a large wrench jammed in the control-rod tunnel.

The helicopter we were flying had just completed a periodic inspection. The maintenance supervisor, a twenty-six-year veteran noncommissioned officer [NCO], had worked his men all night to get the chopper ready for this mission. But his failure to insure that this type of mistake did not occur involved a serious breach of maintenance procedure that could have resulted in disaster for the flight crew, and severe consequences for his career.

Besides my duties as a rescue-helicopter pilot, I was the unit maintenance officer. Misplaced tools left here and there, on workbenches, or in the wrong toolbox were a constant problem. Normally at our maintenance meetings I would hold up errant tools and embarrass the owners by making them come get them before the whole maintenance group.

At my next such meeting, I saved this wrench 'til last. Then I told my group the circumstances under which it was found. This time I didn't have to identify the owner or the NCO. They all recognized the severity of the mistake, and I was confident a lesson had been learned. The proof was in the pudding. There was a dramatic reduction in misplaced tools.

The missing F-101 was located a few days later buried under eighteen inches of snow. The pilot had been killed in the crash.

"PEDRO 05" FROM KAMAN AIRCRAFT "ROTOR TIPS" AT HFI

It was a cold winter day in January 1971 at Zaragoza Air Base, Spain, home of Detachment 15, 40th ARRS Wing. When the Klaxon blared and the alert crew scrambled, Maj. Oger J. VenDange, the pilot, quickly jumped into the cockpit of the HH-43 and flipped the master switch. The helicopter had already been preflighted for an emergency start, so in seconds the turbine engine was winding up and the 51-foot, intermeshing and opposite-turning rotor blades began to whirl.

HH-43 fire-fighting helicopter practicing at Kaman Aircraft Corporation, January 31, 1959. Maj. Richard Kirkland (author) directed the initial training for Air Force crews. (Courtesy Kaman Aerospace Corporation)

Firefighters Sgt. Joseph Walenta and Michael D. Havens, dressed in their "space suit" firefighter clothing, leaped into the cabin of the "Huskie," as did the medical technician, T.Sgt. Larry A. Huchins. When takeoff RPM was reached, VenDange pulled pitch and advised the control tower that "Pedro 05" was airborne. The control-tower operator gave him the runway to be used by an F-86, flown by a Spanish Air Force pilot who had declared an emergency and was about to land wheels up. VenDange positioned himself in a hover near the approach end of the runway and watched the F-86 approach.

Timing his acceleration with the arrival of the emergency aircraft, the major pulled pitch and headed down the airfield slightly behind and above the jet fighter as it swooped over the threshold and hurtled down the runway. When the F-86 touched down, fuel tanks erupted, embroiling the aircraft in a huge ball of fire. Within seconds the HH-43 was over the cockpit of the burning aircraft on the upwind side, blasting down the flames with the tremendous force of rotor wash that intermeshing rotor blades deliver. The pilot popped the canopy, leaped out of the cockpit and into the wash of cool air laid down by the Huskie, escaping uninjured.

The Spanish pilot said afterward that when the aircraft exploded, all he could see was flames, as a searing inferno engulfed the cockpit. He was sure he would be burned to death. Then suddenly, the flames disappeared as did the heat. He looked up and saw the helicopter above him, and it was as though an angel had come to save him.

Coincidentally, the logo of the Air Force Aerospace and Recovery Service (AARS) is an angel holding the world, and their motto is "That others may live." This was only one of tens of thousands of such emergencies responded to by the AARS, in both peace and war, since its inception on March 13, 1946. Originally called Air Rescue Service, it has global responsibility for U.S. military personnel and also conducts a multitude of humanitarian missions. The AARS has utilized all types of helicopters and aircraft for its worldwide coverage, and its crews have been one of the most highly decorated of all U.S. military units.

The Kaman HH-43 was particularly well suited for the crash fire-rescue mission because of the directional channel of high-velocity air created by intermeshing rotors. The high incidence of crash fires in the 1960s and 1970s precipitated the implementation of the HH-43 fire fighting/rescue system. It was assigned to 141 air force rescue units around the world.

"JUMP START" FROM DON BACHALI

It was early spring 1971, and my partner, Steve Wood, and I were doing flight demonstrations in Kettering, Ohio. The chief of the Kettering Police Department, John Shryock, wanted to integrate helicopters into his patrol function. We were there to help by giving demonstration flights to his various commanders and members of the city council who, of course, had to approve the acquisition.

We scheduled flights both day and night, and Steve and I took turns doing the flying. When we finished all the day flights, we took a break and had dinner before the night demonstrations. Shortly before dark, our first passenger arrived in a police car that pulled up and parked next to the playground where the demonstrations were being conducted.

I've forgotten his name, but my passenger was a member of the Kettering city council. He was a pleasant gentleman who was genuinely interested in the details of how the helicopter-patrol system worked. Since it was my turn to do the demonstration, I gave him a thorough preflight briefing and answered his numerous questions. Finally, I got us both strapped in the seat of the Hughes 300 "police" chopper, and we were ready to go. But when I reached for the master switch, it was already on. I knew instantly that it had been left on and that the battery wouldn't start the engine.

Now I had a problem, because I had just finished telling the councilman how reliable this new-technology helicopter was. And if I said I forgot to turn off the master switch, I could imagine him wondering what else had I forgotten. I wanted to be honest, yet not upset or disillusion him.

It wasn't dark yet, so I said to the councilman, "Sir, I forgot to show you one of the special features of this helicopter. Since you have cold winters here in Kettering (they'd had a severe winter that year), I'll show you how to jump start this helicopter if you need to on a cold winter morning."

We unbuckled our seatbelts and climbed out of the helicopter. I then asked the patrolman who was waiting for the councilman if he would pull his patrol car beside the helicopter. He agreed and drove it up next to the tail boom where the battery box on that model was located. I then asked if I could borrow his jumper cables.

Now both he and the councilman were watching me curiously as I attached the cables from the patrol car to the terminals on the helicopter battery. Then I proceeded to show them how, if you had to, you could start this advanced-technology helicopter with jumper cables. Both the councilman and the patrol officer watched me incredulously as I proceeded to start the helicopter, then disconnect the cables and return them to the patrol car.

We then got back in the helicopter, and I flew the councilman, explaining all its features and the concept of police airborne patrol. But the councilman wasn't listening. All he wanted to talk about was the amazing feat of the helicopter getting a jump start from the patrol car.

The Kettering Police Department did procure helicopters for an airborne patrol, one of the many such programs that Donald Bachali directed. I believe the model 300 was the only American helicopter, at that time, with a 12-volt electrical system that could be jump started from an automobile.

"PINNACLE LANDING" FROM RICHARD C. KIRKLAND

When Maria and I were married in 1974, we went on our honeymoon in a little, bubble-nosed Hughes model 300 helicopter. It was a blast. We spent nine days wandering across America the beautiful from coast to coast, enjoying all the wonderful sights you can only see from a helicopter. There were so many exciting experiences, it's hard to choose, but I've always thought this is one of the most memorable:

Monument Valley, Utah, is that place where magnificent pinnacles of rock stand up from the desert floor like ancient sentinels. They are remnants of a land that was once there before millenniums of erosion washed it away.

"Isn't that a fantastic sight?" I said to my bride over the intercom as we approached the valley, flying at about 500 feet AGL [above ground level]. The sun was low on the horizon, which made the pinnacles look even more spectacular by casting long, crazy shadows over the desert.

"It is fascinating. I remember seeing it in western movies many times," she said.

"Yeah. Can't you just see the old stagecoach rocking behind a team of horses as it races across that valley with John Wayne hanging on and shooting at the Indians?" I said, as the full panorama of the valley began to spread across the bubble of our flying chariot.

"Like in the movie, *Stagecoach*. And I remember another one, *She Wore a Yellow Ribbon*."

"One of my favorites."

"Look at that tall, skinny one that goes up so high," she said, pointing to one of the pinnacles that towered above our flight level. "Do you suppose anyone has ever been up on top of that?"

"Maybe a million years ago some Neanderthal guy was up there," I said, banking toward the pinnacle.

"How would he get up there?"

"I'll show you," I said, pulling in some pitch and climbing toward it.

Reading my mind, she glanced at me and said quickly, "That's cheating."

"Maybe so, but look at it this way: we will be the first after the Neanderthal to set foot on it," I said as I set up an approach.

She grabbed the seat and held on. I eased the 300 down over the top of the narrow rock formation, which I estimated to be the good part of a thousand feet high. There wasn't a lot of room up there, but enough to land on. After a little squirming around I got the landing skids wedged into the rock on top of the pinnacle.

I glanced across at my bride. She was watching me with a foxy smile on her face. "You think you're smart, don't you?"

I nodded. "Yeah."

"You're the first one to ever be up here, right?"

"No, the second. The Neanderthal guy was first," I said grinning.

"Uh huh. And did Neanderthals drink beer?"

"What?"

"If you'll look over here, there is a pile of beer cans."

I leaned over and glanced out her door window and, sure enough, there were beer cans! Obviously, someone had been up there since the Neanderthal.

We looked at each other and burst out laughing.

"SWING WING MEMORIES" FROM ROGER SCOTT

When Richard asked for one of my favorite helicopter stories, I found it difficult to pick one because I had so many great experiences in the whirlybird. I finally picked an incident that I still smile over whenever I think about it.

I was a salesman for Hughes Helicopters and was asked to ferry a beautiful blue-and-white model 500 police demonstrator from Newport News, Virginia, to Culver City, California. It was spring 1974 and the trees and flowers were blooming, so I asked my favorite navigator if she would like to go along. Marge, my bride, loved the helicopter and would sneak off with me as often as she could find someone to babysit our seven kids.

We spent the first night in Greenville, Mississippi, where we visited friends. Because of that, we were late getting started the next day, but finally took off and headed west over the "Outback," country that is trees and more trees and a swamp here and there. It was a beautiful day, and we were skimming along in air like glass when suddenly a large bird appeared directly in front of the windshield. I banked away quickly but heard a "thump" toward the rear of the helicopter. Had I hit him?

Although everything seemed normal and the helicopter flew okay, I told my navigator to give me a heading to the nearest interstate highway, just to play it safe. One of the beauties of the helicopter is that you can always land in an emergency. But if we had to land, I wanted to be where we could get a ride.

Marge checked the map and gave me a heading. Awhile later, I intersected Interstate 30 and turned west. I was sure everything was okay, but, just in case, I needed to land quickly I stayed down low and slow over the highway and scooted along above the cars going to Texarkana.

I landed at the airport in Texarkana without incident and couldn't find a scratch on the helicopter. So I could only assume that I'd missed the bird and the thump was my imagination. Since it was getting late, we decided to spend the night and checked in at the local motel. As soon as we'd settled in, we headed to the lounge for a little liquid refreshment.

When Marge and I sat down, I noticed the group of patrons at the table next to us seemed quite excited and animated over whatever it was they were discussing. After our drinks were served, my curiosity got the best of me and I turned around and asked the fellow sitting nearest me what all the excitement was about.

"Haven't you heard?" he said.

I shook my head.

"The route on Interstate 30 from Arkadelphia to Texarkana was tied up by a state trooper in a blue-and-white helicopter patrolling right over the highway. It caused a giant traffic jam. They must'a been doin' something really big."

"Oh," I said, feeling a flush move up my face.

"Yeah. One of the guys is callin' the state police now to see what the hell's goin' on."

I thanked him for the information and, with a red face, said to my navigator, "Hey, look at the time, honey. We better get to the dining room."

"UFO" FROM LARRY CORBIN

Hearing that distinctive sound of beating rotors in the distance, I knew the helicopter was coming but when I glanced to the south, all I saw was this huge 200-foot black glob swinging and bobbing along the bottom of a low-hanging layer of clouds that covered the area. Even though I knew the black glob was the conveyer belt we were replacing in a grain elevator, it looked bizarre dangling out of the clouds. It was attached to a helicopter, of course, but the Sikorsky S-58 was up in the clouds hidden from view.

It was the fall of 1982, and I'd gone out to observe a lift operation that St. Louis Helicopter Airways was performing in the little town of Coshocton, Ohio. Our objective was to lower the belt down the grain elevator. I was in charge of sales and would go out on jobs occasionally to observe. In this case I was sort of monitoring the operation from where I stood in a parking lot next to the elevator. I had on earphones with a mic, so I warned our ground crew the sling load was coming.

Two of the crew, who were on top of the elevator, glanced at the belt that was swinging toward them from out of the clouds. You could just make out the wheels and the belly of the chopper as it approached. I have no idea how the pilot could see what he was doing.

"Okay, you're almost there . . . easy . . . easy . . . forward . . . easy," came the radio instructions from the ground director.

The noise of the helicopter began to thunder down on me, and I could see the rotor wash swirl the misting clouds.

"Give me five left . . . easy . . . hold . . . okay . . . forward three . . . hold . . . down . . . down," continued the voice instructions.

Now the helicopter began to appear out of the swirling maelstrom, and I could see the pilot, his head hanging out the right cockpit window, watching, as the conveyer belt slid down the grain elevator shaft.

"Okay! . . . Hold 'er steady and we'll disconnect," barked the director as the last of the belt disappeared into the elevator.

When the lead line dropped free, the S-58 swung away from the elevator, dropped down over the parking lot, and landed. As the sound of the helicopter died away, it was replaced by the sound of a siren. I glanced toward the highway and saw the flashing red lights of a sheriff's car as it sped into the parking lot and slid to a stop.

A sheriff's deputy jumped out and said to me, "I hope you guys are through lifting that stuff into the elevator. Man I got hundreds of phone calls from all over the countryside about a UFO. They think we got some kind of space invasion goin' on!"

About three weeks later my secretary walked into my office in St. Louis and handed me a newspaper clipping. The headline was "UFO Replaces Busted Conveyer Belt."

14

Rescue at Niagara Falls

I'm a helicopter pilot," said the tall, handsome guy sitting across the table from me in a small café at Niagara Falls, New York. "And I just did what comes naturally in an emergency situation," he added, taking a sip of his coffee.

"You do this sort of thing often?" I asked.

He nodded. "Yeah. I'd say a couple times a month I get a call that someone is in trouble above or below the falls; or they have gone over—in which case there isn't much I can do except fish out the body. But this last rescue was the most dangerous one I've done. It was touch and go there for awhile, and we came close to goin' over the falls."

"Going over the falls?"

"Yeah."

As I recall, it was early fall 1990, and I was visiting David Banks, owner and chief pilot of Rainbow Helicopters, who, just a couple days before, had saved a woman from certain death at the American Niagara Falls. Banks had started his helicopter-tour business back in 1983 and had flown thousands of hours showing visitors the beauty of Niagara Falls. He had also made many a rescue flight in and around the falls with little publicity and even less compensation. He just felt that it was his civic duty to interrupt his sight-seeing business whenever someone was in trouble. When called on, he would do whatever was required, then go back to flying his customers.

I took a sip of my coffee and glanced across at him. "You almost went over Niagara Falls?" I probed, anxious to hear the story.

David Banks in his "Rainbow Helicopter" Model 500 over Niagara Falls, spring 1990.

He nodded, pulled out a cigarette, and fired it.

"I thought you were gonna quit those things?"

He exhaled a cloud of smoke and grinned. "I'm workin' on it."

I grinned too. "Okay. Tell me about the rescue, Dave."

"Well, I had just landed from a tour flight, and my crew was getting ready to load another group when our dispatcher came running out and said the New York State Police called and requested help to rescue a woman who had jumped into the Niagara River and was headed for the falls."

"She'd jumped in the river?"

"Yeah. A lot of folks think that's a cool way to end it all. But when they are about to go over the falls, they change their minds; then it's too late. Anyway, I told the tourists that I'd be back in a couple minutes, pulled pitch, and headed up there.

"It's only a short hop up to the river, and I quickly spotted her, but I couldn't believe she hadn't already gone over the falls. She was clinging precariously to a big rock that was just a short distance from the lip of the falls. I swung around into the wind, set up a hover over the river and inched toward the rock. I could hear the roar of the falls above the sound of the rotors, and the mist began to spray across my canopy.

"I hovered over her slowly because she was hanging onto the rock by her fingernails. I was afraid the rotor wash would blow her off and she would be swept away."

"I guess the river is pretty swift up there?"

Dave nodded. "That it is, and, when I looked down at her through the canopy, I could see by the look on her face that she was terrified and didn't want to die." He shook his head. "I probably got five thousand hours in that bird of mine, and I know what it will do and what it won't. . . . And I knew this was gonna be a tough one, but I had to try. . . . I had no choice."

Banks hesitated a moment, as though he was rehashing in his mind what had happened.

"I eased up as close to the rock as I dared and lowered the left landing skid into the water next to her. The spray from the rotor wash whipping over her face and across the helicopter canopy made it difficult to see, but I could tell that she knew I wanted her to grab the skid. . . . And we both knew she would only have one shot."

Dave and I both took a gulp of coffee, and he took a drag on his cigarette.

"I was fighting the swirling wind gusts coming off the falls and was afraid to put the skid too close for fear of knocking her off the rock. Then she looked up at me, and I could tell she was gonna go for it. When she grabbed the skid, the bird dipped and my instinct was to pull pitch, but I was afraid it would break her grip, so I sort of wallowed there for a second or two as the current swept us toward the crest of the falls. Now I'll tell ya, the current is murder that close to the lip, and I wasn't sure it wouldn't pull us over, helicopter and all."

"Hey Dave, we got customers," interrupted a pretty girl who was the Rainbow Helicopters's ticket taker.

"Okay, I'll be right there," he replied, finishing his coffee and grinding out his cigarette in an ashtray. "It's kinda handy having my heliport right next to the coffee shop," he said, getting up from the table.

"Yeah, but you're not getting out of here 'til I hear the rest of the story," I said.

He grinned. "Not much else to tell. I waited till the last minute, and, when it seemed like we were goin' over the falls, I pulled pitch as gently as I could, and she hung on. I don't know how but she did. Man, she had a death grip on that ol' skid, and she hung on like glue 'til I hovered back up the river a ways to a small island, where a rescue team was waiting."

"Wow! That was one for the books!" I exclaimed.

"Well, I do about twenty-five or thirty of them a year, but not like that one. No one has ever come that close to the falls without goin' over."

"I'll bet she was thankful. What did she say?"

"Nothing."

"Nothing?"

Banks shrugged. "I never saw her again. I don't even know her name. See ya later, I gotta go fly some newlyweds over Niagara Falls."

15

RAID

It was almost midnight when Dave Kickbush nosed his beat-up 1979 Ford into the dirt parking lot of the Alibi Club. He found an open space between an old Dodge pickup and a new Mercedes, pulled in, and shut off the engine. As usual, thc lot was packed with cars, new and old. The Alibi Club was a popular spot with a diverse clientele—quite diverse.

Dave could hear the sound of hard-rock music coming right through the club's brick wall. He hated that music, but it went with the territory of an undercover narc. He reached down, pulled up his pant leg, and adjusted the snubnose .38 in its ankle holster. Then, unbuttoning his shirt, he made one last check of the wire transmitter taped to his chest. All in order and ready for game time.

It was a game Kickbush wasn't crazy about, but it was a challenge that stirred the adrenalin and provided a lot of satisfaction when you won. Of course, winning hinged on everything going down just right and all the players turning in sterling performances. Even then, it was dangerous and often went sour, ending the game . . . sometimes permanently.

As he started toward the club, the sound of a fist slamming into flesh and a woman's cry could be heard over the music. Glancing into the darkness beside the brick wall, he could see a man holding a struggling woman with one hand and beating her with the other. She was fighting back but in a losing effort.

Dave knew from long experience that interfering in that kind of squabble was a no-winner. And it might blow his cover, which would endanger both him and his partner. "Hey! Knock it off!" he barked, staying hidden in the shadows.

"Says who?" slurred the man, letting go of the woman.

"Yeah, mine yer own business," she muttered, obviously inebriated.

Kickbush shook his head and walked to the entrance of the Alibi Club, where a green and red neon beer sign glowed through a dirty front window. The music, and a blast of other raucous nightclub sounds, spilled out as he pushed the door open and stepped inside. The place was packed with an assortment of life gone astray: from little old ladies in sneakers to scumbags who would slit your throat for the price of a fix. It was pathetic and depressing, and when Dave was first assigned to the narcotics unit of the Reno Police Department, it had upset him. He'd worked the streets for years and was no stranger to the reality of street crime, but in the drug world, you really see the dark side of humanity, and the terrible consequences of that business.

Glancing around as he moved up to the bar, he spotted his partner, Richard, sitting at a table in the far corner with a couple of prize specimens of lowlife. Richard was not only his partner, but a friend for many years and had always been meticulous in his dress, didn't smoke, and hated booze. But there he was, playing the role to perfection: dressed like the other dirtbags, swilling beer, and smoking. Then, when Dave got a glimpse of himself in the mirror behind the bar, he couldn't help but grin. He looked even worse.

Well, hopefully they would wind up this bust tonight and get a little break before the next assignment. They had been on this case for weeks, slowly gaining the confidence of a couple of low-level dealers. Tonight it was supposed to go down with a major buy, and, if all went well, they would bag the supplier.

After ordering a beer, Kickbush sipped at it and watched for the signal from his partner through the bar mirror. When it finally came, he lit a cigarette, left the pack next to his glass of beer to hold his place at the bar, and then headed back to the men's room.

Dave stalled in the crowded men's room until Richard entered, then took a urinal next to him.

"Change of plans," muttered Richard.

"What?"

"Activate RAID. Two o'clock at the old Lancers. Blue van."

Richard zipped up his pants and left. Stalling again for a minute or two, Dave returned to the bar, finished his beer, and walked out of the club.

Lt. Kris Kirkland, Nevada National Guard, had just decided it was sack time and turned off his computer when the phone shrieked. He reached across the table and grabbed it.

"Kris, this is Dave Kickbush, we need RAID badly, and we need it quick!"

"Okay, Dave. What's the plan?" asked Kris, snapping his ballpoint pen open.

"We had a major supplier on tap for a drop tonight, but something went wrong and they changed the game plan at the last minute. I can't tell if they are wise to us or just being cautious. At any rate, they are still supposed to make the drop."

"In Reno?"

"Yeah. Two o'clock, out on the Mount Rose Highway."

"Will you have a UC [undercover cop] there?"

"I think so. Richard is supposed to be with them, but something has gone wrong with his wire so we're out of contact. I'm not sure now just how this is gonna play out, so call me as soon as you're off the ground and we'll take it from there."

"Okay, I'll contact you as soon as I'm airborne."

"Thanks, Kris. We can nail some real scumbags on this one, but we're dead in the water without that RAID chopper."

"We're on our way, Dave."

The Reconnaissance Air Interdiction Detachment (RAID) is a unit of the Nevada National Guard in Reno activated in early 1993 for assisting federal, state, and local law enforcement in interdicting the narcotics trade. Relying on the unique features of the helicopter, and its specially trained crews, the unit maintains a twenty-four-hour, seven-days-a-week alert, ready to respond to calls for assistance. Those calls include surveillance of drug-related suspects, command observation, and marijuana-eradication missions.

The crew consists of two experienced helicopter pilots who have received additional training in aerial observation and tracking, both in day and night flying in urban as well as isolated terrain. The RAID crews fly the U.S. Army OH-58A Bell helicopter, powered with an Allison C-20B gas-turbine engine. Nicknamed the "Kiowa," it is small and nimble, with excellent visibility and a high degree of maneuverability, which makes it ideal for the RAID mission.

The RAID Kiowa is equipped with a special radio package for law enforcement communications, night-flying FLIR [forward looking infra red], and a 30,000,000 candlepower searchlight, the SX-16 "Nightsun." Special night-flying and crew-coordination techniques were developed for observation, identification, surveillance, and tracking of personnel and vehicles.

Fifteen minutes after receiving Kickbush's call, Kirkland had driven the short distance from his quarters to the Stead Airport, where the Nevada National

Guard maintains its aviation facility. He had already contacted the facility commander, Major Robert Herbert, advising him of the mission request.

Heavy eyelids disappeared now, and Kris could feel the excitement of the upcoming challenge surging through him as he walked briskly across the aircraft parking ramp toward the darkened shape of the Kiowa. A vehicle-surveillance mission was always challenging, but at night with a big-time drug bust going down, it would be even more exciting and dangerous, and demand a full measure of his and his copilot's skill.

Kris glanced up at the sky. It was a crisp, clear night with a panorama of bright stars across the horizon; a sight not uncommon in the high valley that cradled Reno. Of course, Kris was prejudiced, since he was a true native, but he'd always felt that Reno was the best-kept secret in the country. Oh, it was a twenty-four-hour town, which naturally meant some problems associated with gambling. But there were lots of good, hard-working folks living there, and it was a beautiful little city, nestled in the shadows of the Sierra Nevada Mountains, with the crystal-clear Truckee River bubbling right through the middle of town.

"She's ready to go, sir," said the helicopter crew chief, who had already been alerted by the duty officer and was standing beside the helicopter with a portable fire bottle.

"Thanks, chief. I'll just do a quick walk around," replied Kris. The aircraft had already had a preflight inspection and was ready for engine start, but Kris always took one last look. He quickly circled the OH-58, making sure all the tie-downs were removed and there was no visible damage to the helicopter. Then he opened the cockpit door and pulled his six-foot-three frame into the pilot's seat.

"Shall I start the power unit, sir?" asked the crew chief.

"Yeah, get 'er started. Tom will be here in a minute."

Warrant Officer Tom Watson, the alert copilot, lived a little farther away, so Kris knew that it would take him a few minutes longer to arrive.

When the crew chief gave him the thumbs up, Kris hit the start button, and the whine of a C-20B gas-turbine engine spooling up echoed through the early morning darkness. He watched the needle on the TOT [turbine outlet temperature] gauge swing across the dial then peak out and drop back into normal range. Nice cool start, said the pilot to himself as he released the start button.

He signaled the chief to remove the power cable. By the time he had finished the pretakeoff cockpit check, Watson came running out to the helicopter and crawled into the copilot's seat. Within seconds the pilots had fastened their seat-

Lt. Kris Kirkland (author's grandson) flying a Nevada National Guard 0H-58 RAID helicopter over Reno, summer 1998. (Courtesy Kris J. Kirkland)

belts and put on their SPH-4B crash helmets, which have special attachments for the remarkable AN/AVS-6 night-vision goggles. The goggles resemble miniature binoculars and amplify ambient light 25,000 times, turning night into day.

"The area we're gonna work is out on the Mount Rose Highway, and it will be pretty dark out there, so let's start with the goggles and, if we need it, you can go on the FLIR," advised Kirkland.

"Sounds good, Kris," replied Watson.

Once the goggles were adjusted properly, the two pilots let their eyes and internal senses adjust for a few minutes, then Kris revved the rotor to takeoff RPM and pulled pitch. The Kiowa lifted off the ramp and skimmed out over Stead Air Field and the big white pylon that marked the west leg of the Reno National Air Races course.

"Reno approach control, this is Shadow 89, airborne over Stead," transmitted Kirkland as he put the chopper into a climb and headed toward Mount Rose, which was fifteen miles south.

"Roger, Shadow 89. This is Reno approach. You operational tonight?"

"That we are."

"Roger, squawk 7349. What sector and what altitude will you be working?"

"Looks like the Mount Rose side at 1,500 for starters," replied Kirkland, as Watson set the squawk code into the transponder for radar identification.

"Roger, Shadow 89. We've got no traffic presently, so be our guest. Will advise if something comes up. Good luck."

"Thanks, Reno," said Kris, reaching over and punching a button on the radio console that connected his headset with a special Wolfsburg radio and a mixing system that integrated all the law enforcement frequencies in the Reno area.

"Dave, this is Kris, you up yet?" transmitted Kirkland on a Reno Police frequency.

"Roger, Kris. This is Dave. I read you five square. What's your position?"

"We're coming up over Black Springs, Dave. Be over you in about five."

"Okay. We got an update. Let's go secure."

"Stand by," said Kirkland, switching to a special, secure police channel. Some bad guys use scanners to listen in on police traffic, but they can't pick up a secure frequency.

"Go, Dave."

"The pickup is supposed to be made at the old Lancers restaurant out on Mount Rose Highway at oh two hundred. That's all we know because the plan got changed. Richard is with them, but we got no communications with him, so it's up to you, Kris. Those are bad *hombres* he's with, and, if we lose them, Richard could be in big trouble."

"Okay, Dave. If they show up, I won't lose them," said Kris with a lump in his throat. He recognized the danger to an undercover officer in these conditions.

As he flew the Kiowa along the western edge of the city, Kirkland glanced at the clock on the instrument panel. It was twenty minutes to two. He should reach the spot where the Lancers restaurant had been in about ten minutes and be in surveillance position right on time.

Built on the side of a mountain with a panoramic view of Reno in the valley below, the Lancers had been a popular restaurant until it mysteriously burned down years ago. All that remained now was part of the foundation in a deserted area overgrown with grass and sagebrush: an ideal place for a night drug deal.

Flying with the night-vision goggles is like looking at the terrain in broad daylight, even when it is pitch black outside. As he approached the area at 1,500 feet AGL, Kirkland could easily see the remnants of the restaurant on the side of the mountain.

"There it is, dead ahead," he said to his copilot on the intercom.

"Yeah, I see it."

"Okay, I'm gonna circle around to the west and approach from the south, so that we're downwind of the area. You watch for the van coming up the road."

"You got it," said Watson, scanning the area through his night-vision goggles.

"Kris, this is Dave. You receiving me?"

"Roger, Dave. I read you."

"Good. What's your position?"

"We're almost in surveillance posture."

"Great. Any sign of the van?"

"Not yet."

At 1,500 feet altitude, downwind, on a dark night, Kirkland knew the helicopter was all but undetectable from the ground, even though he was able to see the landscape below as though it was bathed in bright sunlight. And with the use of a pair of gyro-stabilized binoculars, he could pick out a lizard crawling on the Lancers' foundation.

"There it comes," said Watson, when he suddenly spotted the blue van winding up the road that led to the Lancers.

"Yeah, I see 'em," replied Kirkland, then punched his transmit button. "Dave, we got the van."

"Good show. We have units in position along the Mount Rose Highway. Keep me posted."

"Roger."

With the aid of a north wind, Kirkland was able to keep the helicopter in a 1,500-foot stationary hover, which gave him an ideal surveillance position. Observing through their night-vision goggles, he and Watson watched the van pull into the overgrown parking lot and stop. After a moment, three men got out and lit cigarettes.

"Looks like there are three of them, Dave," reported Kris.

"Can you tell if Richard is one of them?"

Kirkland concentrated on the figures. In the green light of the AN/AVS-6 goggles, identifying specific features was difficult, but after a moment of study he said, "Yeah, he's one of them."

"Good. Are you receiving anything on his wire?"

"No. It's dead, or disconnected." Under normal conditions the RAID crew would have been able to hear the transmissions on Richard's body wire.

"Well, at least we know where he is, and it would appear that he is still in their confidence, but keep a close watch, Kris."

"We're on it, Dave, and we'll continue to guard his wire frequency."

Switching to intercom, Kris said, "Tom, you keep an eye out for the drop car, and I'll watch the van."

"Roger."

Ten minutes later Kirkland reported, "Dave, they just got in the van and are headed back down the old Lancers road."

"Double damn! You see any indications of something turning sour?"

"No, it looked like they just decided to go."

"Okay, don't let 'em get away from you. It's vital."

"Don't worry, they ain't gonna get away from me."

Kirkland held the chopper in position and watched the van drive back down the dirt road, dust swirling behind it, then turn onto the Mount Rose Highway.

"They're headed east toward Reno, Dave."

"Okay."

Maintaining his altitude at 1,500 feet, Kris eased into forward speed, keeping the van in sight just over the nose of the OH-58. The van drove down the blacktop highway toward the lower valley. This was easy tracking, since there were only a few cars on the Mount Rose Highway at that hour. Where the highway intersected Interstate 395 near Steamboat Hot Springs, the van turned north toward Reno. Now conditions would change for the RAID crew. Because of all the lights in the city, they could follow the car visually. Both pilots flipped a lever that disengaged the night goggles and stowed them on top of their helmets.

"Dave, they are heading back to the city," Kirkland advised as he watched the van travel toward brightly lit downtown Reno.

"Okay, Kris, you got the eye. All units sector A, hold your positions. Sector B, stand by for surveillance but no intercept. Repeat: No intercept."

The radio cracked with responding narcotics units. Kirkland watched the van begin to mesh with the city traffic. In Reno, automobile traffic is active at all hours, but the RAID crew had no trouble keeping the van in sight as it weaved through the streets. Then suddenly the van pulled into a casino parking garage and disappeared.

"Dave, they just pulled into Harrah's garage."

"Harrah's garage? You think they spotted you?"

"No. I think they're just playing it safe."

"Let's hope so. How long can you stay airborne?"

"I can cover it for about another hour and twenty minutes, then I'll have to refuel."

"Okay. Let's see what happens. All units stand by."

To save on fuel, Kirkland put the Kiowa in a slow, low-power circle around the casino, watching the exits so that when the van emerged, he could again pick up the surveillance.

"Maybe they should go to ground surveillance while we refuel," suggested Watson.

"We may have to do that, but I got a feeling they're not gonna be in there very long," replied Kris.

Lieutenant Kirkland was right. A few minutes later, the van came out of the parking garage and headed down Virginia, the main street in Reno.

"The van has left Harrah's and is headed north," Kirkland reported on the secure radio frequency.

"All right! All units hold until we see which way he's going," snapped Kickbush.

"He turned off Virginia, back onto Fourth Street, and is now headed toward Keystone," reported Kirkland as he maneuvered the helicopter to keep the van in sight, while remaining at an altitude that would make him undetectable.

"Where'd he go?" asked Watson suddenly. The van had entered an underpass-overpass intersection with several other vehicles.

"I don't know," groaned Kris. "He went into the underpass and didn't come out the other side."

"He's got to be in there."

"I think he doubled back, and we missed him."

"How you doin', Kris?" asked Kickbush.

"We lost him. Stand by."

"You lost him?"

"I'll find the son of a bitch," growled Kris to himself, putting the chopper into a circle. "You watch that side, and I'll cover this side," he instructed Watson.

Flying an expanding circle around the overpass, the two pilots scanned the streets and parking lots below. After several minutes of circling without success, Kirkland called Kickbush. "He either got across the railroad tracks and went up into the residential district, or he's parked under the overpass. Have one of your unmarked cars check under there, and I'm gonna head up toward the Skyline area."

"Okay, Kris," replied Kickbush.

Kirkland pulled in full power with collective and headed south. "I'm goin' back on the goggles," he said to Watson. "You get on the FLIR."

"Roger."

The copilot, who sits on the left side of the OH-58, operates the FLIR on RAID missions, using a 9-inch screen. But the pilot also has a small, 4-inch monitor on the right side that he can refer to.

Kris was furious with himself for losing the van. He'd lost targets before, but rarely. And in this case he was agonizingly aware that it could cost Richard his life. He knew these drug suppliers were merciless, and, if they should discover that Richard was an undercover cop, they would kill him without batting an eye.

Then he spotted it.

The blue van was traveling slowly up Skyline Drive, just as he had suspected it might be. Kris breathed a sigh of relief and punched the transmit button on his cyclic. "Okay, Dave, I got 'em. He's southbound on Skyline."

"Jesus, that's great. All units resume plan."

"I got 'em on the screen," said Watson on the intercom. "The way he's driving, I think you're right, Kris. He's just playing it safe."

"I hope so," said Kirkland as he watched the van move slowly through the tree-shrouded residential area.

"Where's he headed, Kris?" came Kickbush's voice on the secure frequency.

"Can't tell yet. He just turned onto Plumb Lane and is headed back toward the freeway."

"Shadow 89, this is Reno approach control. Still no local traffic. All sectors are clear," offered the controller, who, with no air traffic at three o'clock in the morning, was probably watching the zig-zagging OH-58 track on his radar screen.

"Thanks, Reno," acknowledged Kirkland.

"Hey look, he's going onto the freeway south," said Watson, watching the van on FLIR.

"He's headed back south on Interstate 395, Dave."

"Good, good. If he turns off onto Mount Rose, we're on," replied Kickbush.

Silence over the radio for awhile.

"Dave, he went right on through the intersection at Mount Rose and is headed for Carson City," Kris reported, watching the van through his night-vision goggles.

"Damit, something has gone wrong. I can't take a chance any longer, we're gonna have to intercept."

"That will blow the whole deal," said someone.

"I know, I know. But I'm afraid Richard is in trouble. I can't wait any longer. I've got to . . ."

"Hold up, Dave!" Kirkland interrupted. "He just hung a you-ee and is headed back north on 395."

"All right! Stand by all units!" barked Kickbush.

Silence for several minutes.

"He just turned off onto Mount Rose Highway and is headed up the hill," advised Kris.

"That means it's on," said Kickbush. "How is your fuel, Kris?"

"I got about thirty minutes left."

"That should do it. They're obviously playing it safe, but the drop is on, or they wouldn't have gone back up there."

Five minutes later. "He's turned off on the Lancers road," transmitted Kirkland.

"Great. Let me know the minute you see the drop car."

Taking a position on the downwind side, Kirkland brought the OH-58 into another 1,500-foot hover and watched the van drive slowly up the dusty road, and again stop beside the Lancers's foundation.

"You stay on FLIR, Tom, and watch the road. I'll stay on the van with the goggles."

There was no movement at the van for awhile, then the three men climbed out.

"They're coming," said Watson suddenly.

Kirkland turned his head, bringing his goggles to bear on the road, and, sure enough, there was a car coming up the hill.

"Dave, the drop is coming!"

"Unit two and three, get into position now!" barked Kickbush.

A 1980s-model station wagon pulled up beside the van. Two men got out and conversed with the three from the van. After a short discussion, one of the men went back to the station wagon and took out a package. When Kirkland saw the package, he punched the transmit switch on his cyclic and barked, "They got the stuff. Go!"

"Close in now!" boomed Kickbush over the radio, and a few seconds later Kris could see two cars speeding up the dirt road. He lowered the collective and quickly dropped the helicopter to a lower altitude. As the Kiowa came down, both pilots went visual when Tom Watson flipped on the big Nightsun searchlight, which turned the entire area from night to day.

The druggies were caught totally off guard and blinded by the intense light.

Three of them threw up their hands immediately, and one turned in panic and ran head on into the van, knocking himself out. The other one scampered off into the sagebrush. Kris could see that Richard had his Baretta .9 mm pistol out and was covering three of them when Kickbush and the other undercover officers joined him. Two officers went in pursuit of the man who had run off, and the other three were handcuffed. Kickbush and Richard opened the station wagon, pulled out white packages, and held them up like trophies. Their smiles were easy to see in the 30 million candlepower light.

"Hey, thanks guys for the great help," said Richard a few minutes later over the police radio.

"Glad to be of assistance. But I gotta tell ya, I was worried there for awhile," replied Kris.

"Tell me about it. I was wishing I'd listened to you and become a chopper driver instead of a cop!"

Kirkland laughed. "Glad it all worked out. Gotta go, we're low on go juice."

"Hey, Kris, you got time to spot the one who ran off into the sagebrush?" came Kickbush's voice on the radio.

"Sure, stand by," said Kris edging the hovering helicopter over toward the area where the druggie had run. "Get him with the FLIR, Tom."

"It'll be my pleasure," replied Watson, directing the FLIR toward the side of the hill that was covered with heavy sagebrush. After a quick scan of the area, Watson located the missing man, crouching behind a large bush. The glowing heat outline of his body was plainly visible on the FLIR screen. Using the four-way switch, Watson then turned the spotlight on him, and two officers closed in and cuffed him.

"No escape from RAID!" said Kris over the police radio as he rolled in forward cyclic, pulled pitch, and headed for home.

Lt. (now a captain) Kris Kirkland is my grandson and started flying helicopters with me from the time he was old enough to crawl into the copilot's seat. By the time he was a teenager, he could fly nearly as well as I. His desire to fly helicopters with the Nevada National Guard certainly came naturally.

To present the reader with a more comprehensive picture of the RAID mission, I took some liberties narrating this story. However, the details are from my grandson's actual experiences as a pilot and commander of the RAID unit. The Reno police portion of the story came from experiences of Kris's father, my oldest son, who was an undercover narc in his early days with the Reno

P.D. He subsequently became chief of police, then sheriff of Washoe County, and is now the Nevada State Director of Public Safety. Needless to say, I'm proud of both my son and grandson for their contribution to the war on drugs and pleased that my fifty-year love, the helicopter, is playing such a significant role in that war.

16

Above and Beyond

Dan Tyler eased off on the collective, leveling the twin-turbine Bell 412HP helicopter at 5,000 feet, then set power for max cruise and tightened the friction. "It looks mighty treacherous down there," he said over the intercom as he glanced down at the raging whitecaps on the Tasman Sea below.

"Yeah, they were reporting wind gusts in excess of 100 knots and 30-foot swells all through Bass Strait," said flight coordinator and winchman, Graeme Fromberg, sitting next to Tyler in the copilot's seat.

"I have the feeling this is going to be a rough mission," added paramedic Murray Traynor, from where he sat back in the cabin of the helicopter.

"I got the same feeling, and my stomach thinks my throat's been cut," growled Tyler. "Murray, check in my carry-on bag an' see if there might be an old candy bar or something in there, would ya?"

"I already went through everything, Dan. There isn't a scrap of anything to eat in this bird," replied Traynor.

"Okay. So I go a little hungry. It won't kill me, and the poor sailors on those yachts are in a lot more trouble than being hungry."

"That they are. The search and rescue center received eleven simultaneous mayday calls, and I guess one yacht has already gone down with all hands lost."

"It's a real disaster, all right," muttered Tyler. "I hope we can get there in time to save some lives."

The helicopter that Dan and his two-man crew were flying, VH-CFT, belonged to NRMA CareFlight, an emergency medical service based at Westmead

Hospital, Sydney, Australia. The crew had just completed two emergency medical missions that night and, with only two hours of sleep and no sustenance, were airborne again on the most hazardous and difficult mission of their careers—and one of the worst maritime disasters in Australian history.

On December 26, 1998, 115 yachts spread their colorful sails in gentle, midsummer winds and headed out of beautiful Sydney Harbor. Thousands of spectators watched as one of the world's premier yachting epics got under way for the fifty-fourth annual 730-mile race down the Australian coast from Sydney to Hobart, Tasmania. Although warned of testy conditions down course, none of the competing skippers was prepared for what lay ahead.

Late in the afternoon of the second day the fleet sailed into an intense weather depression that had rapidly and unexpectedly formed in Bass Strait off the southeast coast of New South Wales. Hurricane-force winds turned the Tasman Sea into a churning maelstrom with vicious currents and monstrous waves. Most of the fleet was able to reach safety, but the storm struck so quickly that many of the yachts had little chance to escape the onslaught and were disabled. Masts were ripped away as 57-foot yachts capsized and their crews hurled into the sea.

Distress calls filled the airways, and the Australian rescue coordination center called for all available emergency medical and rescue helicopters and aircraft. In answer to the rescue center's request, Tyler and his crew took off in the 412HP from Canberra at dawn and proceeded toward a point 60 miles east-southeast of the Island of Merimbula. They were to back up another rescue helicopter, Polair, en route to lift crew members from the stricken yacht, Midnight Special.

As Tyler listened to the urgent voices on the emergency frequencies, he was suddenly aware of his own call sign: "CareFlight One, this is rescue control, do you read?"

He punched his mic and replied, "Roger control, this is CareFlight One, over."

"CareFlight One, Polair has arrived on scene at the Midnight Special, so we need to divert you to another location where emergency beacon signals have been picked up. Could you respond?"

"Roger control, give me a location," replied Tyler.

"The signals are coming from an area about forty nautical miles southeast of Merimbula."

As soon as Tyler picked up the signals from the emergency beacon he began homing in on the location. When they had reached the area, he lowered the collective and started a gradual descent. "Okay guys, we're in the area, keep a sharp lookout," he said to his crew as they scanned the white-capped, wind-streaked sea below.

After a short search they spotted the ketch, wallowing and pitching wildly in the monstrous waves. "My intuition was right," said Traynor. "This is gonna be a bloody tough one."

"Yeah," muttered Tyler as he banked the 412 around into the wind and lowered his altitude to 500 feet.

"Look at that yacht! It's a wreck. Both masts have been ripped off, and I doubt they have any control," said Fromberg.

"And no radio communication, which is going to make it even tougher," said Tyler, surveying the scene below.

Pitching and bucking in the turbulent waters, the battered ketch, Business Post Naiad, had rolled over twice during the night and had lost her masts, steering, and radios. Her captain and one crewman were dead. The surviving seven waterlogged crewmen clung desperately to the wreckage across her deck, waving frantically.

"From the looks of it, you're gonna need your gear, Murray," said Fromberg.

"I think you're right, Graeme," replied Traynor, pulling on a full-body wetsuit over thermal underwear.

Tyler eased the helicopter down to 100 feet over the floundering ketch. Now the howling surface winds buffeted the helicopter mercilessly.

"What's the plan, skipper?" asked Fromberg.

Dan could see that he and his crew were faced with the challenge of their careers. It was obvious the ketch was doomed and so were the seven crewmen if they couldn't be plucked from the sinking vessel. It would be an extremely dangerous undertaking, and a mistake would mean disaster for all, including his crew and the helicopter.

But Tyler knew he had a dedicated, professional crew who worked together as a well-trained team. He was an experienced American helicopter pilot, having flown Hueys (Bell HU-1) with the U.S. Army's 1st Air Cavalry in Vietnam. He'd met his bride while on leave in Sydney and had stayed in Australia to fly medevac and search-and-rescue helicopters. Murray was an experienced paramedic, having made several overwater rescues in which he'd gone down on the "wire" into the water. Graeme Fromberg was an experienced flight coordinator and winchman. This would be his sixth ocean pickup . . . but never anything like this.

"Okay, fellows, this one is above and beyond the call of duty. So it's your decision, too. We aren't gonna be able to pick them off the boat in this gusting wind and sea spray. The ketch is pitching and rolling so badly, we wouldn't stand a chance, and it's so cluttered with wreckage the cable would probably tangle and dump us all."

"I agree, skipper," said Fromberg.

"Looks like the ball is in my court," said Traynor, pulling on a pair of thermal boots.

"It's your call, Murray."

"What's the alternative?" asked Traynor, fastening the straps to his life vest.

"If we're gonna save their lives, there isn't any."

The young paramedic nodded. "That's the way I see it."

Fromberg grimaced. "I hope we can make them understand they gotta jump off the boat into the water."

"That may not be easy. I'd hate to jump into that God-awful sea," said Tyler as he began to lower the collective, inching the helicopter down. "I'll drop down as low as I dare, and you try to signal them."

With hand signals, Fromberg and Traynor tried to tell the survivors to jump into the water and swim clear of the boat. It was evident they understood but were hesitant to leap into what seemed like certain suicide. But when they saw Traynor in the doorway of the helicopter in his wetsuit, face mask, and snorkel ready to go down the hoist cable, one of the survivors, mounting a good deal of courage, leaped over the side of the pitching ketch.

"One just jumped in, take me down!" shouted Traynor.

"We got live bait!" snapped Fromberg over the intercom, as he activated the winch control [live bait, meaning the paramedic was going down on the hoist cable].

"Roger!" replied the pilot, knowing that now he must apply all the skill and experience he possessed to control the attitude of the chopper that was being slammed by gale-force winds and whipped by vicious water spume.

Tyler had the chopper's nose into the wind, with his eyes glued to the horizon as he wrestled with the controls to maintain a steady hover. In a sense he was flying blind, responding to Fromberg's instructions. In his peripheral vision he could see the monstrous waves swelling to within inches of the helicopter, then falling away into gigantic chasms of turbulent water.

As he went down on the cable, the howling wind spun Traynor around like a corkscrew. Seconds after he hit the surface of the sea, a huge wave buried him in an avalanche of green water, then spit him out the other side in a cascade of white foam.

Wielded by the wind and water, the steel cable, which was his lifeline, now became a slashing, deadly machete as it slackened one instant and snapped taut the next with the rise and fall of the mountainous waves. Fromberg tried to compensate by winching in and out with the rise and fall of the waves, but this was only partially effective.

Fromberg, hanging out the starboard hatch, controlling Traynor's position with the hoist control, kept up a steady stream of instructions to Tyler, whose concentration was now divided between flying the helicopter and responding to the winchman's orders: "Survivor at three o'clock . . . 10 . . . right . . . right . . . hold . . . forward 10 . . . forward . . . hold . . . steady . . . steady . . . left 5 . . . easy . . . left . . . hold!"

In the maelstrom of stinging spray and roaring water below, Traynor was being tossed and jerked through the waves as though he was, indeed, bait on a fishing line. But Fromberg's instructions to Tyler had worked Traynor to within a couple feet of the survivor. Then a huge wave buoyed him, and the cable went slack. Fromberg quickly winched in cable and, when the wave receded, frantically winched it out again.

When Traynor could see again through the blinding sea spray he was within reach of the survivor and grabbed him. He could tell the man was in desperate condition from exposure and swallowed seawater. The roar of the waves precluded verbal communication, but he understood the paramedic's signals to get into the "horse collar," a rescue harness made of buoyant material, that would lift him up into the helicopter.

When he had the survivor fastened securely, Traynor looked up to signal Fromberg, but all he saw was a gigantic wall of water. It buried both he and the survivor, and, in the melee that followed, the cable tangled in their legs. He struggled desperately to untangle the cable before it snapped tight again and left them both without legs.

Looking down from the helicopter, Fromberg saw them disappear under a mountain of seawater. Experience told him to wench the cable slowly until they were free. "Steady, Dan. Steady!" he barked over the intercom to Tyler when he saw them bob up again through the foaming wake. "Okay, right 5 . . . right . . . right . . . steady . . . steady . . . hold! We're over them and I got Murray's up signal, but I gotta wait 'til that next wave passes."

Fromberg knew that if a big wave caught the two men on the cable in midair, it would slam them into the sea with a terrible force, so he must time it just right. At the instant he saw them pop out from under the next wave, he hit the hoist button and pulled them up at full speed, just as the next wave thundered beneath their dangling legs.

"They're coming up, Dan," advised Fromberg, winching the two men, twisting in the wind, up to the hovering helicopter.

When Fromberg told him that Traynor and the survivor were inside the helicopter, Tyler breathed a sigh of relief and instinctively relaxed. Then he was jolted back to reality when he remembered there were six more to go. He couldn't help wonder if he had the strength and concentration to do what he'd just done six more times.

Back in the helicopter cabin, an exhausted Murray Traynor wondered the same thing. But he didn't even remove the winch cable from his harness. He quickly checked the vital signs of the survivor and got on the intercom with Tyler and Fromberg. "He's suffering from exposure and exhaustion, but he'll be all right," he reported.

"What about you, Murray?" asked Tyler.

"I'm beat and waterlogged, but I'll make it, Dan. How are you doin'?"

"It's a piece of cake, Murray."

"Sure it is," said Fromberg.

All three men laughed, despite the awful tension and uncertainty. But each man knew they had to keep going. There was no way they could leave without trying to rescue all the survivors.

A few minutes later, Tyler dropped the chopper down again as low over the waves and sea spray as he dared. When Traynor appeared at the door of the helicopter, the next brave survivor on the stricken ketch leaped into the raging sea. Fromberg lowered Traynor again, and almost immediately he was swamped and battered by the waves as the winchman worked feverishly to keep the cable taut and to put Murray down next to the bobbing survivor. Meanwhile, Tyler fought to keep the chopper in position and respond to Fromberg's instructions: "Survivor four o'clock. . . . Right 10 . . . right . . . easy . . . hold . . . back 4 . . . back 2 . . . hold . . . steady . . . steady."

Again Traynor was smashed deep into the foaming water by a mountainous wave, and again the cable tangled and he had to scramble underwater to untangle it. But he finally attached the rescue collar on the survivor, and Fromberg snatched them from the jaws of another monstrous wave.

"Two down and five to go," gasped Traynor over the intercom as he took a quick breather.

"You okay, Murray?" asked Tyler again.

The heros (left to right), Dan Tyler, Murray Traynor, and Graeme Fromberg, who pulled seven sailors from a raging sea in Australia's worst yachting disaster in history, December 27, 1998. (Courtesy NRMA Careflight, Sydney, Australia)

"I'm just getting my second wind, skipper," replied Traynor. "Let's go, Graeme."

As the winchman lowered Traynor to retrieve the third man, Tyler began to worry about another problem. Would he have enough fuel to remain on station until all the survivors were rescued? If there were no delays and the pickups went as well as they had so far, he could make it. But it seemed too much to hope that nothing would go wrong in this kind of maximum-effort, high-risk operation. And if it did, how in the world could he go off and leave some of those poor sailors to certain doom?

One after another the five surviving crewmen from the Business Post Naiad were fished from the raging sea by the crew of CareFlight One. Each succeeding lift was as dangerous and harrowing as the last, leaving all three crew members exhausted. But after each survivor was pulled safely into the helicopter, the next one leaped into that awful sea, and down Traynor went on the winch, guided by Fromberg, while Tyler fought to keep the helicopter in position until the last survivor was aboard the helicopter.

"Good show, fellows. What say we head for the barn and a cup of coffee?"

said Dan Tyler to his crew as he banked the helicopter northwest and pulled in climb power.

"It was a great effort by a dedicated crew and could only have been accomplished by teamwork, skill, and a high sense of duty," said the Sydney Morning Herald.

I want to add a little to that. I spent many years of my helicopter career doing rescue and medevac, and have seen some brave action by pilots and crews. But I've never heard of a rescue operation where a paramedic has gone into the sea seven times under those conditions and saved seven lives. That was a herculean effort, and, in my judgment, the teamwork, skill, and sense of duty demonstrated by all the crew of CareFlight One was indeed above and beyond.

Daniel Elwain Tyler received the Helicopter Association International 1999 Pilot of the Year award. The crew of CareFlight One was awarded the American Helicopter Society's 1999 Captain William J. Kossler award. The guild of Air Pilots and Air Navigators awarded the crew the 1999 Prince Philip Helicopter Rescue award, which was presented personally by the Duke of Edinburgh. The Australian Government's Bravery and Decorations Council awarded the crew of CareFlight One a Group Citation for Brave Conduct. The Australian National Senate passed a commendation resolution for the crew of CareFlight One.

AUTHOR'S FINAL NOTE

As Igor Sikorsky, father of the helicopter, once said, "The helicopter will bring into the world a whole new means of saving lives." We have seen that prediction come true. The helicopter has developed from its primitive stages of limited capabilities to the present day, where it enjoys all the technological advantages of any other flying machine. It still does not, as Sikorsky also said, compete with the airplane. It is complementary and performs a wide range of important missions well. But none so well as saving lives.